## About the book

*(All functions as they were at the time of the interview. Full interviews available at www.eysinksmeets.com)*

**"I like it. It's provocative to us, especially the part about cavemen in pinstripe. It has got humor."**
Lone Jensen, Business Architect, Jyske Bank, Denmark

**"There is a solid theme throughout the book - the IRR concept, the Value/Compromise model and the PPMMC form a good theoretical backbone for the analysis and the recommendations."**
Schalk van der Merwe, CEO RCS Group, South Africa

**"Easy to read, mind tickling and pleasantly unconventional".**
Theodor Kockelkoren, Executive AFM, the Netherlands Finacial Authorities

**"I like it: jokey style, relaxed way of writing, great analogies, a strong message."**
CEO Global Banking Councils, London, UK

**"Thought-provoking."**
CEO of one of the Scandinavian Banks

**"I thoroughly enjoyed the comparisons with so many other industries ...including porn! I would recommend this book to anyone working in Retail Banking - at all levels and across all jobs."**
Gary Marsh, Head of Retail, Diamond Bank, Nigeria

## About the writer

"He has extensive knowledge of the field, has been all over Europe and is full of examples. He is forthright in his approach, like a real Dutchman, far more direct than we tend to be, and thus very powerful. His style of presenting, his lack of dull reports and his excellent use of pictures and visual concepts gives him a very different, lively style of presenting. He is tenacious, he won't let go, he keeps in touch, he is not willing to accept early defeat and he is ready to say 'I believe you're wrong and I'll prove it."
Hamish Taylor, CEO Sainsbury's Bank, UK

"You can never call in Eysink Smeets too soon. You're faced with a strategic decision but you haven't yet decided what you want. Then it's great to have someone at the table who is as fast as lightning, intensely committed, creative, forward-looking and extremely good at stepping up the pace and broadening the issue."
Hans Hokke, CEO Postkantoren bv (Post Offices Ltd) the Netherlands

"...hire him to shake things up, to determine where you stand, and to show you the way to meet your goals."
Bas Millenaar, CEO, De Hypotheker, the market leading Dutch independent chain of mortgage advisors

"He is highly creative and really looks to the future. He understands and has a razor-sharp vision on what is going to happen in the sector in the next 5 to 10 years."
Hans Hagenaars, CEO Postbank (ING Group), Netherlands

"….he has a unique talent in that he can switch from general strategies to exceedingly down-to-earth astute action just like that…"
Lars Nordström, CEO Nordea, Sweden

"He proved excellent in pinpointing our set of values. He understood our strategy of differentiation and strengthened it, delivered many ideas for converting our soft values into hard values. He is a high calibre ideas generator."
Anders Dam, CEO, Jyske Bank, most profitable general bank group, Denmark

"...we discovered his capacity to look at things from a different angle..."
Olaf Fjell, CEO, Postbanken, large consumer bank group, now part of DBNor, Norway

"He introduced the magic phrase "making things undifficult". And that is precisely what we still do today. making things undifficult: looking at our processes from the interaction between our employees and the customer, and not just from the corporate perspective."
Yme Pasma, Head of Retail, TNT Post, the Dutch national post company in a recent interview, in which he looked back on the start of his relationship with Eysink Smeets

"He is an independent mind who says the things that others don't dare to express, and that is what I love."
Bert van Doorn, Executive, Post Offices/ TNT Post, the mail and courier group, the Netherlands

"Hans is a no-nonsense, hands on type of person who goes straight to the heart of the matter. He'll tell you frankly what he thinks and what you should do and is very direct in his approach."
Dr. Wolfgang Fenkart-Fröschl, chairman of Western Union International Bank

"He knows the sector thoroughly and quickly recognizes what it's all about. Hans is an authority in his own right: knowledgeable, insightful and forward-looking."
Gerrit Grotenhuis, Director Rabobank Enschede, the Netherlands

**Hans Eysink Smeets**

# Porn for bankers.

**Porn for bankers.** What bankers can learn from porn.


Copyright ©:
Short Circuit Publishing BV


ISBN
978-90-817244-4-9


Hans Eysink Smeets
Eysink Smeets Business Consultants BV
Singel 26, 1015 AA  Amsterdam, the Netherlands.
hans@eysinksmeets.com
www.eysinksmeets.com


www.pornforbankers.com

# Introduction.

In this book I write what bankers can learn from porn: Bankers can learn how to change from retailers in sectors like porn, music, books, healthcare, or groceries. All of these sectors fall victim to the Information Retail Revolution: new businessmodels are toppling the old players at a rapid pace.

That revolution is hitting banks. We learn from all these other sectors how new players are winning by offering consumers much more at much less cost and thus much lower prices. Or even for free.

That would be superb for our banks. In spite of all their promises our banks are still not consumer-focussed. Our bankers can rethink their business model, become really consumer-centric, reduce costs massively, which will allow much lower prices. And while they're at it, they can prevent the next crisis too!

I've been active in retail and retail-banking since the 1980s as a strategic consultant. So I know what really goes on within those ivory bank towers.

I don't pull any punches because, let's be honest: without irritation there will be no innovation. But, don't despair: I also offer real solutions too.


Hans Eysink Smeets


P.S. This is a book for bankers, for retailers, marketeers, critical citizens and taxpayers. And on top of that this will give you great ammunition for the next time you run into a banker at a party.

# About the writers

*Hans Eysink Smeets*

Hans is an international retail strategist and has worked as a consultant for retailers and banks in many countries since 1989. Together with his wife and business partner, Karin Montagne, he has been forecasting developments and new trends in retail, retail banking and the consumer-goods industry for over thirty years. The insights gained there form the basis of their strategy recommendations. His work has taken him to 32 countries on five continents and his client base consists of many of the big players.

*With the help of Rik Eysink Smeets.*

Rik is their son. Born into a family which talks retail trends at the breakfast table. Rik has studied digital media design in New York and the Netherlands and developed as an equally sharp-witted unorthodox advertising consultant.

In close interaction with Hans this book was developed, in which the clash between generations leads to new insights.

# Contents.



### Dear Jon*,

The porn sector teaches us that today's retail banking model is at the end of its life-cycle. It also teaches us how you can change your thinking, innovate and rethink your retail banking format fundamentally. It helps you understand the Information Retail Revolution.

It helps you make your organisation consumer-centric. Which creates a win-win situation. Because if the first crisis was caused by mis-selling, a bit of good-selling can do a world of good. At the same time you can cut costs. Create a new balance between direct and face-to-face channels. Put retail-sense into your corporate and investment colleagues. And, last but not least, you can do your bit to prevent crisis no.2!

Isn't that nice?





### The Information Retail Revolution.

Every retailer in information is now retailing in bits & bytes. That's why the Information Technology Revolution is followed by the Information Retail Revolution.

That's true for porn, music, travel, dating, gambling. And, yes: that's true for banking as well.

The Information Retail Revolution not only destructs old formats, it initiates innovative new tools and formats too.

# How would Apple do banking?

Winners of the Information Revolution like Apple or Google could be thinking about banking. Maybe they are developing it right now. Maybe it is just days away from introduction. Who knows? Does it scare you, Jon? Or does it inspire you?

These new information giants breath the rules of the Information Retail Revolution every day, and have shown to be able to expand their expertise into new territories time and time again.

Let's see how they might apply that knowledge to financial services.





# Bankers? Cavemen in pinstripe.

Good-selling can do a world of good: increase consumer satisfaction, lower costs and help prevent the second banking crisis too!

We all know that unprecedented levels of mis-selling (product-customer mismatching) caused the first crisis. Mrs. Consumer got a mortgage she couldn't afford. That became the first stone to topple. Which toppled many more stones, a process that got jet-powered by the IT revolution. Which in turn led to the toppling of the global system in the first crisis.

Changing the way you sell makes perfect sense.

**The need for re-inventing the retail model.  75**

# Branches and trust.

Innovation in retail banking wasn't the hottest item on the agenda right after the crisis. In spite of the new found love that bankers have declared for safe and boring retail banking.

Banks are now stuck with eroded branches, all-time low customer trust and still too many bankers that didn't learn a thing from the crisis.

Retail bankers share their branches dilemma with porn-kings, record-stores, and travel agents:

"What to do with the damned branches... we can't do with them, we can't do without them... and they are getting costlier every week".



**Selling kitchens is like selling financials.  101**

# How would Ikea do banking?

Ikea from Sweden has revolutionized furniture retailing in the past decades. They have liberated Mrs. Consumer from the claws of pushy, bonus-driven salesmen in shady furniture stores.

One sector still escaped their consumer-centric approach: kitchens, one of the largest and scary decisions in any household. Until recently it was assumed that you could not sell a kitchen without knowledgable advice from salesmen.

Ikea turned that conventional wisdom on its head. With great success. And with many parallels with the financial sector.

> Ikea could sell financials even better. *102*
>
> Ikea and heavy financial products. *103*
>
> Ikea took the 'scary' out of it. *105*
>
> Ikea does it with a few stores. *107*
>
> Ikea is the same world-wide. *109*

**From caveman to modern lover. 111**

# Modern match-making.

Banks should put all effort in the matching process which comes before the actual sale of the product. It's where most impact can be made. It is where most things went wrong. It is where most costs in today's banking are coming from.

> Modern romance brings productivity. *112*
>
> How healthcare matches the right pill to the right person. *114*
>
> While you were busy cleaning up after the crisis. *116*

**Learn from Information Retailers.117**

# IRR rules that would do banks a world of good.

Many lessons from other Information Retail sectors can be applied to retail banking.

It will make your bank go from mis-selling to good-selling. The Information Retail Revolution makes this possible on a massive scale at low cost.

Use the lessons from the Information Retail Revolution lessons to help you prevent crisis no.2.

> Information Retail Revolution Rules. *118*
>
> No Compromise is the main trend. *119*

# How Jyske Bank does banking.

As we have seen now, the rules & tools of the Information Retail Revolution are not just a threat. They are the key to success in retail future. By applying them yourself you can change your retail banking fundamentally. It will put the consumer first. It will enable good-selling. It will reduce costs. Like I've demonstrated with Apple and Ikea.

In this chapter we show you how these rules come together in the present too. In a Danish bank that has already adopted many of these learnings.

**Learn from hard-core retailers. 181**
# Supermarkets and banking.

Yes, supermarkets are getting more active in financial services in lots of countries. Bankers can learn from their integrated consumer-focus. By applying their huge consumer-trust and high contact-frequency they may become an impressive competition to banks, Jon.

But -good news for you- we also see a lot of supermarket banking initiatives that fail to get off the ground. Or crash soon after take-off. Or exit after a few years. Why? Most get too far outside their comfort zone. Which disturbs their normal consumer-intuition and decisiveness.

All in all: some lessons from supermarkets for bankers, Jon.



**Keep the playing field level. 201**
# Other sectors have regulators too.

Bankers tend to complain about the strict regulations and compliance rules. Even more so after the crisis. But rules and regulations keep the playing field level in any economic sector.

We don't dislike that as consumers. We like it that an independent authority looks after our interests in food, medicines and cars.

Why would it be any different when it comes to our financial needs?

The Information Retail Revolution is here to stay. Exploit the new tools and conventions it offers. Not only out of defensive reasons. Use them to innovate and go on the offense. The benefits can be enormous.

Learn from other sectors how to create a larger footprint, with more sales power, at far less cost. And prevent crisis no.2 too.

What are we waiting for? If now is not the time to rethink your business model, when is it?



## And:

* *Jon is the CEO of a retail bank, or Head of Retail in a universal bank. He could be anywhere in the world. We wrote this book as if we were writing to him. Are you, reader, a retail banker? Just copy/paste your own name instead of Jon. Are you an interested outsider? Then understanding Jon will help you understand how a retail banker thinks. And how the Jon's of this world influence your life. We ask the questions that Jon would ask. Plus the questions that Jon should have asked, but never did. And we give Jon our honest answers.*

# Introduction.
# Dear Jon*,

The porn sector teaches us that today's retail banking model is at the end of its life-cycle. It also teaches us *how* you can change your thinking, innovate and rethink your retail banking format fundamentally. It helps you understand the Information Retail Revolution.

It helps you make your organisation consumer-centric. Which creates a win-win situation. Because if the first crisis was caused by *mis-selling*, a bit of *good-selling* can do a world of good. At the same time you can cut costs. Create a new balance between direct and face-to-face channels. Put retail-sense into your corporate and investment colleagues. And, last but not least, you can do your bit to prevent crisis no.2!

Isn't that nice?

# Why bankers can learn from porn.

Porn for bankers?! Yes, Jon, you retail bankers can learn a lot from porn. You can learn from porn how you can be a much better banker. Be more consumer-centric. Do all of that at much lower cost. And -if you're lucky- you can prevent crisis no.2, while you're at it.

Why porn? Maybe not the most politically correct thing to say, but porn has always led new developments in new media since the invention of book printing. Porn is information-retail. The IT-revolution has turned all information into bits & bytes. That revolutionised the way porn is created and produced. But also the way porn is distributed and sold. Most business in porn has shifted to the internet. And that's true for banking as well.

You can learn how porn found a new balance between their IT-driven channels and their brick & mortar outlets. Porn has found that the need and function of brick & mortar outlets is reduced and revolutionised. True for banking too. Porn shows that the Information *Technology* Revolution has led to an Information *Retail* Revolution. Porn has found new tools and conventions which are now standard in many information retail sectors. Portals, customisation, channel-mixes and much more.

But don't worry, it won't be a sleazy book. I have used insights from many other information-retail sectors too.

Once you understand the Information Retail Revolution, you will understand that this created the first crisis. And by thinking along these lines you can prevent crisis no.2.

It tells you what you should do with your damned branches. How -after the 3 year strategic paralysis because of the crisis- we can restart the fundamental rethinking of your multi-channel retail formats we were working on before.

Yes, Jon, we can achieve a greater footprint, have far higher consumer-satisfaction, have more sales-power and save 50% or more on the cost of your network at the same time. Wouldn't that be nice?

In these pages I share our new, sharpened insights with you. In the style that you know from me: in Q&A's. The Q's came from the retail bankers I encountered in the past months. And I added the Q's which I think you retail bankers should have asked, but didn't.

As usual, I write in stark black and white. You know that the grey-tones in between will present themselves in the course of our discussions.

Kindest regards, Hans Eysink Smeets

**Porn for bankers.** What bankers can learn from porn.

## Why porn, music, books and banking have lost their bearings.

# The Information Retail Revolution.

Every retailer in information is now retailing in bits & bytes. That's why the Information Technology Revolution is followed by the Information Retail Revolution.

That's true for porn, music, travel, dating, gambling. And, yes: that's true for banking as well.

The Information Retail Revolution not only destructs old formats, it initiates innovative new tools and formats too.

# Porn and the missing stores.

### How did you get the idea of using porn to solve strategy issues for us retail bankers?

*I got the idea during my daily walk to the office.*

As you know Jon, my office is in a 17th century canal house on one of our beautiful Amsterdam canals. When I am not travelling around the world, I take the train to work. I get out at Amsterdam Central Station for a nice 10 minute stroll to the office.

Amsterdam has a red light district. The streets leading away from our station used to be littered with porn-shops and sex cinema's. Not unusual around the world's central stations. Well, those porn retailers are gone. The porn shops are replaced by hip sandwich shops, ethnic supermarkets, and coffee shops. Just two porn stores are left on my stroll. Both lead a sorry and meagre existence. All that is left for them, is selling some DVD's, toys and lingerie to tourists.

### What happened?

*The porn stores fell victim to the Information Retail Revolution.*

Information Technology has revolutionised the way porn is made and distributed. Most of the products the porn industry sold were mere *carriers* of porn. DVDs, videotapes, magazines. With the obsolescence of these carriers, the IT revolution spilled over into porn *retail*. The stores disappeared. The Information Retail Revolution was then a reality. Conventional brick & mortar outlets closed their doors.

This *Information Retail Revolution* is now making casualties in many sectors. Not only porn has trouble with branches. So do post offices, cd-stores, games-outlets, travel agents and many many more sectors. And retail banks, Jon.

# Porn always pioneers new media.

**Why on earth are you picking something sleazy like porn out of all these examples of Information Retailers?**

*Porn always pioneers the way into new media.*

It is not the most political correct thing to say, but every new medium that was invented throughout the ages was instantly noticed and exploited by the porn sector. Porn then pioneered the commercial use of these new media. Time and time again.

Gutenberg invented book-printing? Porn adopted his new communication technology immediately and pioneered new and interesting ways to earn a buck. Photography started? Porn found new commercial models with it instantly. Videotapes, Minitel, CDI, DVD, 0900-numbers, mobile phones, the internet? Porn pioneered the way to make the new technology accessible and commercially viable.

New conventions pioneered by porn, quickly found their way to other sectors.

You may find it untasty, but it makes sense to study the porn sector when revolutions in media are happening. Learn the rules, the new conventions, and then see if you can trace these new developments in music, film, books. And retail banking.

Sorry, Jon, but that's reality.

# A new sector: Information Retail.

**Information Retail? I thought we bankers were in Service Retail.**
*Yes, you were. Not anymore.*

Many sectors are moving into Information *Retail* rapidly. All because the Information *Technology* Revolution has spread and spread. It has crept into more and more parts of the value chains of many sectors. And as IT moved into and replaced many phases of the sales process of service and products, the sector definitions changed.

We now acknowledge Information *Retail* as a new playing field, with its own set of rules, and with its own winners and losers.

**When did that all happen?**
*Fairly recently, Jon.*

Porn stores used to be retailing printed media and DVD's. Tangible stuff. Atoms. Porn has gone *bits & bytes*. Which allowed them to change channels. From brick & mortar stores to the internet. With some brick & mortar stores left for tangible merchandise.

Porn suppliers have made it easy. You no longer have to visit a sleazy shop with your head covered under a big hood anymore. You don't need to mumble what your preferences are, or the title of the movie that you are looking for. No more sneaking out with a crumbled paper bag. They have become Information Retailers. Their retail outlets are websites on the internet. The internet allows you to find your preferences immediately and go straight to your individual and differentiated interests.

That is a substantial improvement. You weren't too proud of leaving a porn shop with a big pink box that says 'Miranda' and a stack of magazines and DVDs with luminous titles all hidden away in a brown paper bag.

But what about the blow up doll Miranda? Isn't her whole purpose to be tangible? Sure, but until the post man hands Miranda over in a discrete brown pack, Miranda is, like the movies on the DVDs, just information, bits and bytes.

That is the first lesson from porn shops. They sell information. **Anything that can become bits and bytes, will.** And when that happens, invariably the Information Retail Revolution will hit not much later.

## Did this revolution influence prices too?

*Yes. It offers more value, at much lower prices.*

A decade ago the porn industry produced 10 thousand official titles per year. Now, there are millions of movies made every year. From formal *and* informal producers.

Anyone can make a porn movie, and anyone can watch it, from anywhere. In many cases totally free as well. That is another lesson from the Information Retail Revolution: **if it can be free, it will be free**. The porn sector's earning model has crumbled. Rearguard fights to defend old earning models are invariably ineffective.

Once again, if these things happen in the porn sector: other sectors beware!

## How are things now for the porn industry?

*Many have suffered badly from the effects of the Information Retail Revolution. It ruined their earning model.*

The original earners suffered. The consumers have a lot more to choose from, and much of it is *free*. Simply because the production of porn has shifted from a small elite towards the masses. Up until the mid-nineties, there was a distinct separation between the production and consumption of products. Selling identical products to an audience that is not involved in the production process, that is how you earned money. That has been key to mass production since the Industrial Revolution.

You put your stuff for sale on an anonymous market. That's why your products should meet a -potentially boring- average of tastes. Customising and differentiation was impossible, you needed large runs. Spontaneity and individuality lost out to accessibility and cheapness.

Many people still view the world as such, and for years this went well. Until recently. The Information Retail Revolution made a power shift possible. New media and technologies are responsible for the change of the anonymous mass market into a heterogeneous, critical -and above all- self-producing group. That is what other Information Retailers can learn from porn: **everybody is a producer.**

All of this is killing the earning power of the porn industry. It creates rapidly changing business models. Let's see what it did in some other sectors.

# Music and the Information Retail Revolution.

**Can we go into some less sleazy examples, Hans? Music has been hit by the Information Retail Revolution too, hasn't it?**
*Yes. With the same devastating effect.*

Music was a thriving business where four big players dominated the world. Sony BMG, Universal, Warner Bros and EMI. They used to make the products, they owned the artists, they owned the only earning model. Models that were based on expensively produced albums, followed by long promotional tours, costly artist publicity and video-clips, plus -last but not least- printing millions of silver discs. In exchange the labels got loyal consumers that would buy these discs. We would massively buy the CDs sold in record stores. Artists would set out on worldwide crusades to promote them.

That is no more, as we all know.

**Any idea of the numbers involved in the changes in the music industry?**
*Yes, Jon, let's go down memory lane for a bit.*

Remember *Thriller* by Michael Jackson? A dazzling 29 million copies were shipped to retail stores in the USA back then. An estimated 65 to 110 million copies worldwide. That not only made it a No.1 hit in the USA for 37 weeks, selling 1 million US copies in its best week, it made it one of the best-selling albums ever.

By contrast, today's harsh reality: while I was typing away on this book I heard on the radio that Cake's *Showroom of Compassion* was the new No.1 *album* in the USA in the last week of January 2010. Cake sold an all-time low of 44 thousand copies to reach that glorious No.1 position.

By contrast, the no.1 *single* in that same week of January, 2011 sold 400 thousand copies. But those were downloaded. Bad news for music-stores, I guess....

**Yeah, I see why the music industry is in trouble then.**
*Absolutely torpedoed by the Information Retail Revolution.*

They are not only struggling. Their business models are ruined. The figures I just gave were only the legitimately downloaded numbers. But who still buys singles or CDs? No-one. **If it can be free, it will be free.** One more of the Information Retail Revolution-rules that you retail bankers must learn.

New technologies have made it possible to send out music into the world, and to share it with anyone online. Without (the formerly profitable) interference of the labels. This has caused a major power shift towards the masses. It creates a dynamic and producing society. But brings bad news to the labels: it knocked down their existing business models.

**Will the former music giants fight back their way into power?**
*Unlikely.*

Instead of adapting to the Information Retail Revolution, and thinking up new ways to sell their music, record companies are fighting the new developments with lawsuits. They prove another Information Retail Revolution rule from which you retail bankers can learn: **old earners defend instead of innovate.**

The attacks of the IRR on their business model were dubbed *piracy* or *digital theft*. The labels are fighting their desperate rearguard defensive actions and resisting ferociously. But new power-houses like iTunes have adopted the new rules of the Information Retail Revolution. They are taking over.

David Draiman, songwriter and lead singer of the US band *Disturbed*, in a response to one of those massive US lawsuits brought on by the music giants. "The focus of the industry needs to shift. It's the way of the future. You can smell it coming. Stop fighting it, because you can't."

He wasn't the only one. Artist and producer Moby commented on his website: "File sharing is a reality, and it would seem that the labels would do well to learn how to incorporate it into their business models somehow.

(..) Record companies suing 12-year-old girls for file sharing is kind of like horse-and-buggy operators suing Henry Ford."

## Does this Information Retail Revolution hit the brick & mortar CD stores?

*Massively. Check your HighStreets and shopping malls.*

Virgin Megastores, which started in 1976, has folded in many countries. They make no secret of the reasons on their own site: "*....times they are a-changin', and sad but true - Virgin Megastores are no longer open in the UK, Ireland, Spain, US, Canada and Japan...*" Only HMV has survived in the UK until today, but is rumoured to hang on by their economic finger nails. And may have dropped by the time you read this book.

Record companies and CD stores merely sold the tangible *carriers* of music. And because they have built their retail formats around that, they are now close to extinction. Music is nothing but Information. That is why they are swept away by the Information Retail Revolution.

Banking, Jon, is nothing but Information too.

# Gambling.

**Are there any examples where the Information Retail Revolution has given a new lease of life to brick & mortar outlets?**
*Gambling seems an exception.*

On-line poker seems to be putting new life into casino's. Hundreds of thousands of people play poker on-line each night. You would expect casino's to be wiped out as a result. Like porn shops. But the casino's don't seem to suffer as badly.

I talked to a friend, professor in economics, recently. He is an enthusiastic and pretty good poker-player in his spare time. I asked him if on-line gambling is making casino's indeed as obsolete as porn shops.

"Hmm.., ", he answered, "..interesting question. But no, I don't think so, casino's are more busy than ever. I played an international poker tournament recently in Las Vegas, on invitation, all expenses paid, because I performed so well on-line. On-line poker tournaments lead droves of gamblers to the casino's. Which would mean that the total gambling market must have grown considerably."

**I guess the conclusion that the Information Retail Revolution blows away all brick & mortar outlets is not always true then?**
*It seems so, although it may be too early to tell.*

I receive conflicting information. Las Vegas is in deep trouble, so are other casino's. Is it fatal? Or a new lease of life? The gambling sector, just like the porn sector, has always shown great agility and adaptability to exploit new trends. It takes agililty and adaptability to grasp the new multi media opportunities.

How do retail banks score on that front?

# Cars.

### Okay, music became digital, but what about a sector that sells tangible goods? Like cars?

*The Information Retail Revolution hits the retail infrastructure of cars as well.*

Where do you go when you want to buy a car? Dealership? Wrong. Of the somewhat bigger cars, the lease-segment, at least 50-60 percent of the new cars are sold, yes, indeed, by a lease company.

That's not all. You orient yourself for a car on the internet. You compare prices there. You customise your new car there. Get your discounts there. We can find a lot more information about the car online than a salesman in a dealership can ever offer you. The asymmetric relationship of the past -he knew immeasurably more than you about the product and the prices- has vanished.

You only go to a dealership for the test drive. But those costly salesmen and showrooms carry pre-IRR cost levels. The lease companies squeeze the retail prices. Even worse: a dealership doesn't make money on the sale of a new car, but on products and services in its life-time. And what does the lease company do? Send their customers for all that additional business to dedicated chains. Dedicated chains for tires, for glass fitting, for accident-repair, etc.

What car manufacturers are now retailing to you, is *information* about cars. Many phases of the sales process that once were the domain of a dealership, and which were the fundaments of their business model, now happen on internet. Their earning model is in deep trouble.

Car dealers have become a showroom for the lease companies. That's turning their business model upside down. Time for car companies to completely rethink their networks.

**Could we imagine the same scenario for us bankers? Could our bank-branches be reduced to just show-rooms, or advice-centres for mortgages or pensions? Which are then bought online elsewhere?**

*Yes. It's happening already today.*

Your clients are using your advisors, exploiting them for their advice, using them to make up their mind. Then they go home, use the price-transparency of the internet to find the lowest price, and buy it there. Leaving you with lower and lower conversion rates.

It has happened in home electronics, travel and hardware. There are no reasons for it not to be happening in banking.

**Not everybody buys a new car via a lease company. Most buy second hand.**

*There it's even worse! That market has been hit by the Information Retail Revolution even harder.*

Look at eBay and its national equivalents. They have sucked up the second hand car market massively. So called p2p (Peer To Peer) trading goes on, without a middleman. Another Information Retail Revolution lesson: **p2p trade: if you can cut out the middleman, you will.** Are we sad about it as consumers?

# Travel.

## I get your drift, Hans. Isn't travel another good example of the Information Retail Revolution?

*It is, Jon. Have you booked a holiday lately?*

For us consumers, the fact that information retail is going through a revolution is a huge improvement. Remember going into a travel agency? Remember the plastic beach balls and paper palm trees? The middle aged woman behind the desk? That's how we used to buy holidays. That's over now.

Why? Because travel agencies don't sell *holidays*, they sell *information* about them. They are in *information* retail. Another IRR-rule: **rethink what you are really selling.**

Nowadays, we go online, look at a couple of websites, compare, read reviews and then book our flight and hotel directly, or through a portal, a mark-up website, such as Expedia or Booking.com. Almost all phases of a travel process have become digitalised; selection, choosing, purchasing, boarding, complaining, everything.

The only thing that is tangible is the flight itself. Just like the inflatable doll at the brick & mortar porn shop.

## Can travel tell us how rapidly things can change?

*Yes. Think of Booking.com.*

Only 10 years ago a businessman from the East of Holland started this hotel-booking site. Today he is market leader world-wide, has immense buying power with the hotels, and is present in 130 markets. Such a speed of global expansion was unthinkable in the old travel agent business, where *bricks & mortar & people* just took so much more time to expand.

# Books and movies.

### The eBooks are coming. What will happen to bookstores? The next victims of the Information Retail Revolution?

*Without doubt. It's happening right now.*

And it will proceed with increasing speed in the next couple of years. The people at Barnes and Noble probably still claim that people come there for the nice atmosphere, the wise staff and the good coffee. And probably some do. But most people just want to buy a book. Or better: something to read. Or better still: something to spend some nice hours with.

The immense choice and the ease and interactivity of book selling sites like Amazon has created a forceful competition. The next phase is starting now: electronic books to read on Apple's iPad, Amazon's Kindle or on the pc. With software like Adobe Digital Editions. These new companies don't have to change their corporate culture to understand the rules of the Information Retail Revolution. They breath them day in day out. They apply rules like **p2p reviews**, or **personal recommendations by using analysis of your previous behaviour** in a natural way. Once again two new rules of the IRR which can and will be applied in many sectors.

Including banking, Jon.

### And the video rentals of movies?

*Suffering the most of the Information Retail Revolution right now.*

Video rental chains are collapsing. MGM, Sony and Blockbuster are in bad shape. We consumers only need the movie, we won't bother with the carrier, the DVD, if we don't have to. And that's why transporters of any kind of information are suffering greatly. Once the compression techniques plus the power of computers allows it, films will become as versatile as music.

# Communication.

### Post offices?

*Only kept alive by governments and unions.*

Mail is hit massively by the Information Retail Revolution. Volumes dropped by huge percentages in recent years. Have you send a letter lately? I haven't. Post offices are crumbling in front of our eyes for that very reason. If they still exist in *your* country, it is because your government and unions keep them open. In the same way that our banks are kept alive with artificial respiration.

In a country where the market really rules, like the Netherlands, they are closed within just a few years.

### Telecommunication?

*Vodafone is an excellent example of how new technology-driven players can outperform and destroy old ones.*

Vodafone started in 1985, its origin in Racal, a company manufacturing military telecommunication equipment. They won one of the two mobile phone contracts in the UK, and went on to become the largest global mobile phone provider. Leaving many of those old telecom-giants green with jealousy.

And where is the old telecom now? Brick & mortar phone booths are dismantled world-wide right now. Land line telephony obsolete in many countries. All replaced by mobile phones.

But even the mobile phone industry is under attack of the next cycle of the Information Retail Revolution; people call and text each other for free on their smart phones, using third party media like Ping, Viber, Whatsapp, Facebook or Skype. Will Vodafone be agile enough to survive, or go the way of the music giants?

### Can we learn about cost reductions from the telecom world?

*Yes. Certainly.*

Our national (formerly state-owned) phone company KPN has reduced its staff from some 33 thousand some years ago till about 10 thousand right now. The value of their offering to the public has increased tremendously, but the forceful competition has not allowed them to chalk up the cost-reductions as profits.

If only, Jon...

# Dating.

**Well, all of the examples may be true but banking is about relationships. That's completely different, isn't it?**
*Know what happened to dating?*

Dating is all about relationships, it has been hit completely by the Information Retail Revolution. What does a single person do in 2010? Of course: go online. It used to be something you didn't talk about, but online- dating, just like online-, well, *anything*, has become totally accepted. It just works better. So even the oldest market there is in personal relationships has been hit massively by the Information Retail Revolution.

That's unromantic, you might say, but with statistical certainty you have a much better chance to find the love of your life.

My son Rik has a female friend in her twenties, who dates around 2 new guys a month. But -hey- not just some guys she picked up at the bar, she does it through internet dating. The Information Retail Revolution offers her a much more efficient and focussed process.

At that bar, she may find 150 people. That seems an impressive number, but half of them are male, around a third are of her age. That leaves 25 people. Then she has to filter out the ones that already have someone, the ones with crazy hobbies, smelly feet, thin hair, too low, or too high education, different interests, and so on. That doesn't leave her a whole lot of choice out of those 150 people in that bar.

Online, a really smart matching system easily filters out her 2 guys from 100 thousand men. That would be impossible to achieve in any other way. Think about the hours and money spent, and beers drunk before she has seen a 100 thousand guys at a bar. She would be a homeless alcoholic before she finds love.

That is yet another lesson you retail bankers can learn from the IRR: **electronic matching systems** have become accepted. And -even better- preferred.

# Retail banking.

**Got your drift, Hans. Will banking be hit by the same Information Retail Revolution rules as porn, music, film, cars or dating?**
*Yes. Exactly the same. It's happening right now.*

Banks were in service retail. They are in information retail now. Banks trade in information. We now know that all information inevitably becomes bits and bytes, and that the Information Retail Revolution will follow not much later. Retail banking will be forced to follow the rules of the Information Retail Revolution. Or else!

The Information Retail Revolution is raging all over the world, it's not bothered about sectors or borders. There is a real danger that Retail Banking will react too slowly to avoid the huge impact of this Information Retail Revolution.

It may even spell the end of the life time of banks-as-we-know-them. Why not? Many sectors have a 100-year life time. Just think of trans-atlantic steamers and mass-market department stores.

The times of sub-optimizing your retail banking business model are over, Jon. Playing around with polishing tiny details of your business model is dangerous.

And you better speed up. We are not talking about the long term future. The Information Retail Revolution is happening right now. Rethink or get out while you can. Wipe your slate clean of all your business models of today.

Re-invent your business from scratch.

## Learn from the new information giants.
# How would Apple do banking?

Winners of the Information Revolution like Apple or Google could be thinking about banking. Maybe they are developing it right now. Maybe it is just days away from introduction. Who knows? Does it scare you, Jon? Or does it inspire you?

These new information giants breath the rules of the Information Retail Revolution every day, and have shown to be able to expand their expertise into new territories time and time again.

Let's see how they might apply that knowledge to financial services.

# Apple iBank.

**What would Google or Apple do if they would go into banking?**
*Start something like iBank.*

If Apple or Google were to start iBank, they would apply the lessons of the IRR. That would not feel difficult or alien to Apple or Google; they *live* these rules & tools every day.

They would go for an intermediary function like they have with iTunes, iBook or the AppStore. They will embrace the fact that banking products can be made by anyone. You, me, the traditional banks. iBank would sit between them all, like the intelligent matching system that iTunes or Appstore is. They would encourage anyone to make and offer financial products. Exactly like they do in their App Store. It is also likely that they would enrich the financial assortment with some basic products of their own too.

**With iBank, banking would become like an open source marketplace? With an assortment of financial products like the AppStore?**
*Yes.*

iBank would sell FinancialApps, just as it sells iPhone or iPad Apps. With strict rules, governed by Apple. Which is quite funny, as most financial authorities in most countries do not check financial products before they come onto the market. Wouldn't you like that for financial products too, Jon?

**What is an App? I don't have an iPhone or iPad.**
*An App is a little bit of software, a program for your iPhone, iPad or other smartphone.*

It can be bought via the AppStore, the online store in iTunes. Which you enter through your laptop, mobile phone or iPad. The AppStore assortment consists mostly of third party software. Games, informative programmes, newspapers, navigation software, everything. Following the Information Retail Revolution principle that everybody is a producer, thousands and thousands of developers now fill the assortment for this new medium.

This assortment is not a jungle of unreliable Apps, but governed by very tight rules. Apple sets these rules. It's their environment, their brand. They aim to preserve quality. They aim to prevent rip-offs as much as they can. Last but not least it creates their earning model: Apple gets a share of each App that is sold. The AppsStore has created a whole new economy.

iBank would do exactly the same.

### Say I need some money to buy a car. How would iBank work?

*Just go to iBank on your computer or smartphone.*

In the intuitive Apple environment that you are familiar with, you will be able to select your solution from a transparent assortment of all kinds of financial products. You hit Transport. Hit Car Loan, and see all the offerings, the financial Apps, if you will.

Just as you know from iTunes or the AppStores, the FinanceApps are organised into different genres, different categories. FinanceApps like Revolving Loans, Fixed Loans, or P2P loans. And probably the new inventors of FinanceApps will discover new, more intuitive, more human categories. Just as you are familiar with Jazz, Soul and R&B in iTunes.

The price setting of the FinanceApps apps is done by the producers, not by iBank. They may choose to offer fixed, flexible or actionable prices. You select the Apps which seem to fit your requirements, check out the ones you like, read reviews of other users, see the star rating.

Then you may buy it.

### Will people buy complicated financial products on iBank? Can iBank offer advice?

*Yes. With all those normal tools of the Information Retail Revolution, that we all have learned to trust.*

Structured information. Previews. Reviews. Do-it-yourself analysis through Q&A's. Or the Genius method: an analysis of previously purchased products. *"...if you liked this product, you will probably like this one:..."*

### Can they help me find my personal risk profile too?

*Yes. With the RiskProfiler App.*

They would use all the by now usual Information Retail Revolution-tools. Like activate a new RiskProfiler App to analyse other applications on your computer, like mail or Facebook. By doing that this App may give you your risk profile instantly. That process is called *text-mining* and can use patterns of repeating words to analyse how your mind works. That would not have to be a threat to your privacy, because it could be done in the sheltered environment of your own PC.

When it returns your profile, you would be able to communicate just that profile, not the process that went on before it, to the world outside your computer.

### How can I see the implications of the car loan?

*You would use the familiar concept of Preview, that you find in many Apps.*

Can the loan level out the big cost wave of that car, or will I get in trouble later? An App called iWaves could help you calculate payments into the future and shows you the potential risks or opportunities. You have a play-by-yourself area, which you can save in a private area, until you activate it with purchases. Like the shopping cart function on Amazon.com.

### Can iBank help me understand the impact of my decisions on my financial future? That is what a bank advisor is for, isn't it?

*iBank can do that job much better.*

*iBank would offer the simple iWaves App to help you understand what your financial future life will be, based on today's situation. Each of your LifeEvents causes ups and downs in your income wave and/or your cost waves. A financial product really does nothing but help you level out those waves of your financial life in time. It would be great if the waves of your costs could be completely in synch with the waves of your income. But alas, that is seldom the case.*

If you buy a house, it creates a huge financial wave, of a size that can never be synchronised with the much more modest wave of your income of that month. That is why you take on a mortgage: it levels out that huge wave of the purchase of your house over many, many more months. It prevents you from being washed over by the costs of the house.

Financial products level out the waves of costs today into the future. Or they create a reservoir with which to level out upcoming waves of costs.

Think of the levelling out of the financial waves of your entry to university. Your first job. Your marriage. Your first baby. Your second baby. Your promotion. Your new car. Your inheritance. Your bonus. Your house. Your retirement. Every LifeEvent may need you to level out your life's waves. Planned LifeEvents or unplanned LifeEvents.

### Can iBank organise my complete financial life?

*Yes. Along the same familiar lines.*

In iBank in the familiar left hand column of your first window you will find the normal categories of an average person's financial life: Pay, Budget, People, Transport, Home, Pension, Invest.

iBank has windows of the main normal LifeEvents with pre-settings, which you can personalise as you like. Just like you are used to in many other programs. iBank offers different angles with which you can look at the same data. Just as in iTunes.

From there on you can make your iBank as customised as you want it to be. Something which was totally alien 10 years ago, but which is now perfectly feasible and follows well-known conventions.

# iBank face-to-face advice.

**But banking products can be scary. I need a 'trustworthy uncle', who can lead me through this scary period. iBank can surely not offer that?**

*Yes, they can. Apple today has a channel mix that can do just that, and with which we are completely at ease.*

Computers are expensive items, bought with a low frequency and packed with hard- and software we don't, and will never, know anything about. In essence, buying a computer can be as scary as a financial product. Did I pick the right one? Did I not pay too much? How do I customise them to my precise needs? Wouldn't you like a 'trustworthy uncle' to help you through the scary process?

Apple provides such trustworthy uncles. They make it easy. Actually, they make it fun. Apple does have brick & mortar stores too. With face-to-face advice from real people. To help you through the scary or insecure phases of the purchase or use of your hardware or software.

**Why do you need stores when you have such a good IT system?**

*You need the right mix of Information Technology and Information Retail.*

Everything can be bought online, but that doesn't mean they strip down the stores. On the contrary. They work together.

What you see at home, is what you see in the store. One system, that also the employees plug into. And most importantly, you get instant satisfaction.

## So these stores are about experience?

*No!*

Experience is a popular buzz word. But it's nonsense in most cases. People want to be served with quality products that help them. That's a real need.

An experience is never a real need. First serve need. And banks still have enough to learn about that. If zero would be the minimum accepted level of serving a need, banks would be below the line. Once you've mastered that to level 10, then you can think about experience.

## It's funny that a bunch of IT geeks from Apple understand brick and mortar so well.

*Their corporate culture is consumer-oriented by nature.*

That's why a large company like Apple forms a big threat to you retail bankers. They are the masters of programming complicated systems and make them behave in an intuitive, consumer friendly way. They are equally good when it comes to brick and mortar retail. They have an intuitive understanding of what makes people tick. They use their IT background to advantage. They take the knowledge out of the people and put it in the IT. For everybody to use. That doesn't make Apple dumb. It makes them confident and smart.

# iBank multi-channel advice.

### Does Apple offer advisory services?

*Yes. They perfectly understand the 'trustworthy uncle' principle.*

Apple products can be bought online. They provide online 'trustworthy uncle' tools with customer reviews, blogs, discussion sites and analysing tools. But go to one of their Apple stores and you'll experience a well oiled machine with huge amounts of employees walking around. With flesh and blood 'trustworthy uncles'. Or better, *'trustworthy nephews.'*

Unlike bank advisors, Apples trustworthy nephews are not programmers of computers. They are hired because they can deal with people. And they seem to know everything. The wisdom of these people is not in their heads; it's in their hands, in the shape of an iPad. They've got tools. Screens. Unlike their bank colleagues.

In an Apple store you have your discussion with constant visual support of a monitor. The advisor is not hidden behind the screen, with you helplessly staring at the empty back of it. Which is the unhappy convention in banks. No, you are both at the same side of the screen, sitting next to each other. You bounce your discussion via that screen. The screen offers direction and visual support to the conversation. We call that phenomenon screen-bouncing. A convention that we are all used to. Apart from the ease and speed of the discussion, it creates a great equality between the advisor and yourself. It takes out the uneasy asymmetry that is so normal between advisor and consumer in banking.

The Apple store is designed to make the most of the human factor in the advice process. People walk into one of the huge Apple stores to get help at the Genius Bar, or get inspired at a seminar on making movies. Or pick up their kids from a photo editing class.

In the Apple store, you can do everything yourself, but when it gets complicated, when you need to be enthused, or need a soothing hand on your shoulder, an Apple employee is often standing right next to you. Apple knows the 'trustworthy nephew' principle.

### But in finances we have all these legal issues to tend to?

*See how Apple tackles their many legal issues today: Integrated.*

They go for instant satisfaction. Contracts and conditions are integrated in their software. Identification is tackled in the same easy way. That is necessary in the purchases you make in iTunes or the AppStore.

Apple does everything that enables you to settle the deal right then and there. And makes it fun, just like they do in their stores now.

### Why is it so much fun?

*They show you what you can do with their product. Not how it works.*

A computer is as boring as a financial product. A computer is an enabler. Just as a banking product. But they *both* enable you to do incredibly exciting things. Your computer can open up a completely new life. A banking product can do that too.

Bankers tend to explain how their products works, bore the customer with technical details. Just as a bad PC-salesman will bore you to death with bits, bytes and hertz. Mrs. Consumer will have sweaty armpits and a headache when she is done talking about that mortgage.

Apple talks about the cool things you can do with their products. Take photos, share them with your friends, make a movie, and even your excel sheets look awesome on an Apple computer.

They understand that an iBank mortgage buys you a dream house. They make the dream process great fun. That is how iBank makes banking exciting.

# iBank private banking.

**Apple iBank can do mass market financials in this way, I guess. But for our private banking clients this will surely not work.**
*Nonsense. For them it is even more attractive.*

Your private banking clients haven't become wealthy by living in the 19th century. Apple is used to working with 15-year-old kids as well as small and medium sized business owners and also with filthy rich private persons.

Just think for a minute of your 35 year old private banking clients. What would they prefer? Vague back-of-the-envelope advice in walnut-clad meeting rooms with pinstriped bankers, where the coffee is served in silver pots by softly speaking young ladies from good backgrounds? Or would they prefer the informal, fun, modern, highly effective instant satisfaction of iBank?

Private banking cries out for the same fundamental rethinking, if it wants to ensure a sustainable future.

# You can do what iBank can do.

### In which country is Apple online with iBank?

*None.*

I made it up. But they easily could. My main message is: if Apple can think iBank, so can you, Jon.

### Apple will not do iBank!

*Maybe they will, maybe they won't. But the main question is: will you do it, Jon?*

Maybe Apple is working on iBank right now. Maybe they haven't even thought about it. Maybe they did and rejected the idea. Maybe somebody else is working on it right now.

But what is most important: does the threat of Apple iBank scare you? Or does it inspire you? Do you feel that they may be much better than you conventional retail bankers? Yes? Then do it yourself, Jon.

### Why Apple?

*Because iBank would be right up their alley.*

They are a company based on the lessons of the IR Revolution, they know how to deal with shops and people, they know how to orchestrate their phases in the buying process (IT vs real people), they have a huge amount of customer trust (which you didn't even have before the crisis, for that matter) and they could make a lot of money with that move.

Imagine an Apple bank opening up in your neighbourhood. Scared? Or inspired? I guess I have made my point, Jon.

# Don't downplay the iBank threat.

**It would take years before Apple or Google would have all the ingredients of such a bank ready. That would allow us banks to change our show.**
*Wrong, Jon. Don't downplay this threat.*

All of what we have described uses very normal technology and very familiar conventions. For Apple. For Google. For the consumers. Not for you bankers.

Much of this is pretty alien to most people within your bank. Hard struggles will need to be fought by the few of you who can think the iBank way. You know the uphill battle of convincing hardened, conservative bankers. Many of whom are still convinced that the ultimate, but unreachable dream for Mrs. Consumer is to have her own pin-striped personal banker in a walnut-clad office, talking softly about technically advanced, yet incomprehensible *haute-finance* products and taking discrete notes with his gold-tipped fountain pen on his expensive note pad in its calfskin-leather cover.

Recognise this, Jon? Changing the minds at the top of your bank takes time. That'll take the bite out of these concepts for these banks, and -last but not least- will allow others to enter first.

### What is it that Apple would bring to the party?
*Brand trust. Freedom of thinking. Speed of development. A natural use of all the Information Retail Revolution lessons.*

Apple doesn't have to think twice about understanding the IRR-learnings.

They have created many of them themselves. And used that wisdom to great effect in a constant flow of new innovations. Whether it's hardware or new applications, they breath IRR.

And they constantly enter the next territory with it. After iTunes and its Apps-store, Apple has now announced that they will start a software store on the internet. Different from all other software stores on the internet, Apple will give you full 100% brand trust: it will be easy, with a very intuitive and recognisable interface, and very reliable.

**Apple or Google are in computers, phones, internet stuff. We're in banking. That is a trade they don't understand.**
*They're not in internet stuff. They're in information retail; e-mail, cars, mobile phones.*

These companies surround us all day long in many ways. They understand the rules of the Information Retail Revolution like no other. Leave it to these companies, that established these rules, to make the next move into yet another new territory. And when they do, they'll have a huge advantage. They'll start from pole position, without the burden of huge legacy systems and costly branch networks.

But my aim is not to do Apple's job, it is to make you change your game fundamentally, Jon.

**Do you seriously predict a threat from that side, or are you just writing some shocking statements to juice up this book?**
*I'm serious. The potential of such a thing to happen is way too big to neglect.*

I'm not saying it will be Apple, Google or Microsoft, but it's not that unlikely. They could reinvent the whole sector in years while that would take you decades. Why is it that Google is making the first self-driving car, and not one of the car manufacturers? It's because Google starts from a human interaction point. They are so used to think in a human manner that they've cut off years and years of pre trajectories.

Plus, they're IT people. Setting up the most people-friendly banking system won't be hard for them. It's at the core of what they do.

**What would be the impact if Apple entered the financial markets for real?**
*Huge. They would sweep away most conventional banks.*

Just as they did with iTunes. The old music conglomerates are totally subservient to Apple now. Losing more and more of their function each month. Being replaced by do-it-yourself musicians and new music publishers who breath the rules of the Information Retail Revolution.

Just as iBook or Amazon.com will sweep away the old publishers of books.

### Would Apple have to enter in one huge big sweep?

*Not necessarily. They could dribble it in as well.*

They could start with a FinancialApp here and there. See what it brings them. Then take the next little step; the next App. And the next. And the next. It will be no problem for Apple to get a bank license. But why would they have to get a bank license? They can distribute iFinance in the same way as iTunes. Not their own products, but a commission from the producers instead.

### You know that these giants have their failures too? That Microsoft has pulled back from MS Money?

*Yes, we know.*

Microsoft had in MS-money a rather outdated vehicle, which was closed in 2010. It lacked the simplicity that iTunes or Appstore offer. It had too much advice, too much of the old routines of the conventional banking world. It was overloaded with add-ons meant to generate extra revenue. Which made MS money slow and confusing. But don't be sure that they will not give it another try in a new format anytime soon.

But even if they don't, stop spending valuable breath on their failures. Look at their successes. And spend all your time on *your* new successes. Think like them and change your bank, Jon.

**Bankers and relationships?**

# Bankers?
# Cavemen
# in pinstripe.

Good-selling can do a world of good: increase consumer satisfaction, lower costs and help prevent the second banking crisis too!

We all know that unprecedented levels of mis-selling (product-customer mismatching) caused the first crisis. Mrs. Consumer got a mortgage she couldn't afford. That became the first stone to topple. Which toppled many more stones, a process that got jet-powered by the IT revolution. Which in turn led to the toppling of the global system in the first crisis.

Changing the way you sell makes perfect sense.

## Bankers are like cavemen in pinstripes.

**Well, Hans, I think we agree that we are not as consumer-focussed as Apple would be, when we build a relationship with our clients.**

*That's an understatement, Jon. When it comes to relationships bankers do not behave as modern lovers, but as cavemen in pinstripes.*

The banker's notion of a relationship is not unlike the romantic ideas of the caveman. He sees a juicy victim, hurriedly shoots out of his cave, doesn't take the time to get to know her, pretends that she is in for a long, intimate and romantic relationship, after which he hits this starry-eyed consumer over the head with the product-of-the-month, drags her to his cave. Ready!

Another notch on his club, yet another victim. And these pin-striped cavemen really believe they have created a relationship for life.

**Isn't building a relationship with our clients our core-business? Our reason for living?**

*Yes, so you all promise. But only few deliver.*

Banks promise Mrs. Consumer a relationship for life. But in fact bankers have the romantic instincts of a caveman. Maybe your bank is the exception, Jon. Then you're lucky.

But at most banks I know, this is the reality.

### Do we bankers really promise romance-for-life?

*Yes, you have and you've started doing it again, Jon. On a grand scale.*

Here are some banking mission statements or ad slogans from right before the crisis from a number of banks:

*"To offer our clients state of the art service in their financial choices for the future."*

*"Individual treatment. We treat you as we would wish to be treated ourselves."*

*"We want to be your home banker with service that makes the difference: always personal, where and when you want."*

Well, yes, those were heady claims, weren't they? The same type of claims start creeping in once again.

### Are we really selling the product of the month, rather than the consumers needs?

*Of course you are. Your product-of-the-month follows the natural tidal movement in banks.*

You sell loans, when you've got a bit too much money sloshing around. You sell saving when the money tide is running low. And that's why you sold credit, when credit was cheap.

Or looked cheap in the rosy glow of that time.

### Can we bankers live up to the promise that we know you?

*No. That's an exception.*

The client believes that her bank knows her. But her bank knows only part of her at best. And in reality it is more a question of: "Eh, what was your name again?" And when you get back after two years you can forget all expectations. Do you want that from your home banker?

Does that lead to a long relationship? Does that lead to good advice?

### Can banks live up to the promise of a file on you?

*Limited. And your soft data are lost anyway.*

Often there is a field called 'soft data', or 'notes', or 'other'. What to put in that field is up to the individual advisor. He can put 'soft data' in on your life, your family, your visions for the future. Or he can put nothing in it. More often than not 'soft data', or 'notes' is more like a garbage can for data. Incomprehensible for anyone but the advisor who typed it in.

But in most cases this field does not contain any data because of lack of time. Most data that banks collect is aimed at improving CRM efficiency, not at getting to know the client better.

### Does the -inevitable- transfer of clients go well?

*No.*

If you have done your story with Mr. 1, you can start all over with Mr. 2. Mr. 3. Call centre 4. Mrs. 5.

Sounds familiar, Jon? Or is your bank the lucky exception?

# Caveman behaviour caused the first crisis.

**Isn't this caveman-behaviour the result of the crisis?**
*No. It's what caused it, and you know it Jon.*

I have told this caveman-story since 2001. It illustrates in a simple way the fundamental flaws in banking: the structural lack of even the most basic desire to understand the client, the structural mis-selling, the lack of consumer-focus. There are a few exceptions, and maybe your bank is, Jon.

But even in my wildest dreams I didn't foresee that this cavemen-attitude would lead to the toppling over of the global financial sector.

**When you tell the caveman story to these bankers, what is their usual reaction?**
*A sniggered laughter of recognition.*

No banker has ever objected to my comparing him to a caveman. In fact most feel rather proud & macho about it! Nobody disagrees, in fact everyone recognises and confirms what I am talking about.

Invariably I could note a touch of nervousness in their laughter; the laughter of admitted guilt. Or, to put it better; the embarrassed laughter of being caught out. There was a trace of pride in their laughter too; pride at being a hunter.

**After you tell the caveman story, does a good discussion start among these bankers on how to solve these problems?**
*Rarely.*

What happens much more frequently is that when the sniggers die out, *cavemen* stories start to bounce around the table. One banker tries to outdo the other with even wilder cavemen examples. It resembles the pride that prevails at meetings with car-salesmen too.

# Don't blame your advisors in your branches.

**Who is to blame for the caveman behaviour? Are our advisors in the branches stupid or -even worse- evil?**
*No, Jon. It's you guys. The top of the bank.*

The people that I meet in the branches of banks in many countries are hard-working, intelligent and doing the best they can. Yet they are forced into a painful split.

They *know* they have to behave like cavemen. They *know* they cannot build a relationship with their customers. They *know* that their knowledge of their customers is at best sketchy, at worst non-existent. They *know* that this can lead to an imprecise or even wrong match between the product and the client.

They *know* that they have to mistreat the customer. They *know* mis-selling occurs. They *know* that this might cause a nuisance. They *know* that in some cases it may cause something more than a nuisance. That their cavemen romances can cause serious problems. They *know* it.

They are constantly stretched between what is required of them and what is realistically possible.

What they didn't know, until the crisis, was that this caveman behaviour could be lethal. What they didn't know, is that this mis-selling, this lack of proper matching, would contaminate the global financial system. Not in their wildest nightmares could they envision that it would topple the financial system in so many countries. There is no doubt that the structural caveman-like mis-matching caused the lines of domino-stones around the world to topple.

Don't blame your advisors in your branches, Jon. Blame yourself. And act now.

# The split caused the crisis.

### What started the crisis, Hans?

*Mis-selling did it, as we all know, Jon. It started that global toppling over of huge amounts of financial domino stones.*

A story we all know by now. People were sold these so-called *sub-prime* mortgages. Mortgages which didn't fit their financial life.

That process has been euphemistically called *'mis-selling'*. Salesmen, without interest in the financial life of Mr. & Mrs. Consumer, did that *mis-selling*. Sometimes they were driven by their own greed, their commission. Sometimes they did it to reach their sales-targets. Sometimes they did it because otherwise the bank next door would sell it. And too many times it brought the bank-advisor in that painful split. A split between mis-selling and good-selling really. But in most cases the saleman didn't have the tools and/or the time to get to know his customer.

Not surprisingly, there came that awful day that Mr. & Mrs. Consumer couldn't keep up with the monthly payments for their mortgage. Their inability to pay each month spread and spread, till it reached global proportions.

It's a familiar story by now.

### So we agree that not all bank advisors are crooked sales-men?

*It wasn't always because of sinister or cynical reasons.*

The wide-spread justification that Mr. & Mrs. Consumer could pay the monthly costs was based on an overly optimistic fairy-tale, built on a very optimistic cumulation of very optimistic scenario's happening *all* at the same time.

This economic fairy tale was believed and shared by many in the industry. Therefore, more or less cynical *mis-selling* was totally acceptable daily behaviour.

### Which collection of economic fairytales did you come across around the world?

Here are a few of them, in random order:

*1. Credit was cheap, and would stay that way.*

The interest that Mr. & Mrs. Consumer had to pay each month, would stay nice and low. Credit was cheap. And would stay that cheap forever and ever.

That was quite optimistic thinking in itself.

*2. House-prices were going to go up indefinitely.*

Their bank allowed Mr. & Mrs. Consumer a loan that was worth as much, or even more, than their house was worth. But who cared in those hazy days? Mr. & Mrs. Consumer might be hanging on by their fingernails in the first years, but the security under their loan was going to be grow and grow and grow, and life would get easier and easier with time. Paying back the mortgage later on would be a piece of cake. Mr. & Mrs. Consumer as well as the bank would live happily ever after.

Rather optimistic scenario too.

*3. Shares would stay up.*

Often shares were advised to Mr. & Mrs. Consumer as the preferred tool to save their money in. The performance of these shares would make their piggy-bank grow and grow and grow. And when it got time to pay back their mortgage, the brilliant performance of the shares would have filled their piggybank to the point of overflowing. Because, as the general accepted fairy tale commanded, shares were going to go up. And up. And up. Indefinitely. Yes, Mr. & Mrs. Consumer would be looking forward to a very nice retirement indeed.

Once again: a rather optimistic scenario.

*4. Local currencies would keep their value.*

In quite a few countries the mortgage was not in the local currency, but in foreign, sexy, hard, currencies like Swiss Francs or Japanese Yens. Your local, unsexy, soft currency charged a much higher interest, and you would be a fool to pay that. Nobody mentioned the currency risk. Or maybe someone just mumbled about it. Mr. & Mrs. Consumer didn't comprehend the concept of currency risk anyway, or just for the duration of the sales-meeting. The harsh reality was that the amount they had to pay each month was based on the exchange rate between their un-sexy currency and the sexy Swiss Francs.

That this exchange rate would stay the same forever after, is yet again a rather optimistic scenario.

*5. The government would pick up the risk.*

In countries like the USA the government was strong on stimulating home-ownership. That resulted in a wide-spread understanding that the government was -at least- agreeing to the credit craze, and there was even the implicit trust that they would pick up the risk involved. How they would do that, differs per country, but by turning the interest rate knob, the government, or the central bank, would be able to keep these nice market conditions under control & nice.

Well, that politicians can change their tune, shouldn't come as a big surprise, now should it?

# The domino-stones toppled all down the line.

**We agree on the story so far. But the damage wasn't done completely at the front line, was it? That's not what toppled these gigantic banks world-wide?**

*We agree, Jon. It was the securitization, the trade in packaged mortgages through your back-doors.*

But what made those packages unstable? The unstable mortgages that were sold at somebody's front door made them unstable, right Jon? Banks packaged the individual mortgage of Mr . & Mrs. Consumer together with many others and traded them world-wide. A process which we know by the name *securitization*. Funny name; '*securitization*', because it suggests that this packaging is indeed '*secure*'. These apparently very secure stacks of mortgages were then sold to other parties. Information Technology gave that trading unbelievable speed and allowed these securitized packs of mortgages to be traded at the speed of lightning around the globe.

These securitized packages of mortgages were cut up, repackaged, resold, cut up, repackaged, resold, repackaged, until nobody had a clue how many mis-sold mortgages were really in those massive stacks of mortgages.

The traders in these packaged mortgages understood that there were contaminated mortgages in these packs. But as nothing went wrong, the definition of risk faded. The traders knew that a certain percentage of these mortgages were contaminated as the result of mis-selling. But as all scenario's were optimistic, and the good times lasted longer and longer, the appreciation of the mis-selling risk got less and less. Nothing happened to them, eh? Why worry?

# Why the mortgages were sold on.

**Maybe a good moment to explain to our non-banker-readers why we retail bankers sold our mortgages on? We didn't do it just for fun, did we?**

*Good point, Jon. Let's try to make a bit of your high finance understandable for laymen.*

You didn't want to hang on to the mortgages at all. You asked your investment colleagues some floors up in your bank to sell those loans out the back door as quickly as possible.

Why? It's because you are forced to put a certain percentage of every mortgage amount into your safe, and close the door tight on it. The regulator *requires* that you put that *capital* in your safe. That phenomenon is called, yes, indeed: *capital requirements*.

You are not overly happy with that, because all that fine *capital* just gathers dust in your safe. It's dead money. The regulator forbids you to do anything even remotely risky with it. Which is not unreasonable; it's there as a back-up in case Mrs. Consumer is unable to pay her mortgage back to you. Because you want to be able to pay your *savers* back, whose money you used to give Mrs. Consumer her mortgage. That's the basis of banking. Capital requirements guards the money of your small savers, but also the huge ones like pension funds.

All you retail-bankers were looking for methods to put that dusty capital in your safe to more profitable use, weren't you?

**Very much so. I agree so far. Perhaps explain to our non-banker-readers how we liberated that money?**

*By selling on your mortgages.*

When you sold a mortgage to a Mr.B, Mr. B owned your mortgage from then on. And he therefore owned the risk too. Hurray! That's when the regulator allowed you to open up your safe and take that dusty *capital*

*requirement* money out. You blew the dust off, and started earning money
with that capital again.

**The regulator allowed me to take out that capital, because when
I sold on the mortgage to Mr. B. I no longer owned that risk.
That's fair isn't it?**
*Yes. Ultimately the risk was Mr. B's headache. But there's more to it.*

In the beginning the management of the mortgage you sold to Mr. B
remained at your bank. That was the phase when you, as the original
salesman, were still very much interested in the changes of quality of
those mortgages.

Later on US regulators put an end to this by calling what you did a trick
and told you that when you sold the mortgage to Mr. B, it was Mr. B's
headache from there on. *Out of sight, out of mind.* That's when you retail
bankers started to lose interest in the quality of your sold-through
mortgages.

That led to both you and Mr. B losing track somewhere.

**Weren't people worried that Mrs. Consumer could get into
trouble paying back her mortgage?**
*Well, if it went wrong you'd phone Mr. B and he'd have to cough up the
money.*

But to be honest: no-one worried much at all. Nobody really foresaw
much trouble. The *rating agencies*, those large world-wide companies,
that rate *what* risks *what* financial instrument carries, were seen as the
ultimate referees. They put most lights on green, so neither you, nor Mr. B
worried too much.

But transparency about the risk of that first domino-stone got confused
and lost along the way. Because Mr. B sold the mortgages on. He remixed
and repackaged them and sold them on to Mr. C. Who did the same
remixing trick. And sold it on to Mr. D, who sold it to Mr.E, who...,well,
you get the picture.

That is how unrecognisable bits of your original mortgage to your Mrs. Consumer ended up with Mr. Z in Tokyo at the touch of a button. It was hidden away, unrecognisable, overnight.

Still agreed, Jon?

**Agreed. Ultimately the health of these packages of remixed mortgages in Tokyo remains dependent on the health of that mortgage of my Mrs. Consumer, right?**

*Exactly.*

How well she (and all those millions of other Mrs. Consumers) payed back their mortgage or credit card is at the core of the health of all those securitized packages of mortgages. That is the domino-effect.

Nobody disputes that simple fact, Jon. But that simple fact got rather fuzzy in the confusion since the crisis, don't you think?

**Could these securitized packages of cut up and remixed mortgages enter our bank via the back door again?**

*They did, didn't they, Jon?*

Your investment friends in your bank, a couple of floors up in your office building, traded in these securitized packages of mortgages just as everybody else did. Almost nobody could resist the temptation. They didn't have a clue what really was in there either, and/or put to sleep through attractive Triple-A labels from the rating agencies.

# The IT Revolution accelerates the problems.

### Why did this all happened now?

*The IT revolution accelerated the spreading of the toppling domino stones.*

Selling mortgages long-distance was pretty difficult before the IT-revolution. Then call-centres and internet came along. Automated credit-scoring, without the personal assessment of the salesmen became more and more possible.

That is how IT accelerated the mis-selling. But IT accelerated the spreading of the toppling global mortgage market too.

Before the nineties, large-scale and fast global trade in financial products was still pretty difficult and expensive. Then the IT-revolution kicked in. It jet-powered international trading of financial products and dropped the costs.

That is totally unlike the German meat traders who at least had to wait for the trucks to drive from one warehouse to another. Now mortgage traders zap the huge packages of contaminated mortgages around the world at the push of a button.

### Summarising, Hans: we cannot blame the crisis purely on my mortgage salesmen, can we?

*Agreed. It was a sector-wide domino-game.*

But the quality of the world-wide lines of domino-stones starts with the quality of the matching process in your front-line. That is no new insight as such. But preventing these first stones to topple and with them the next crisis, gets disgustingly little attention.

That irritates the hell out of me, Jon. And -as we know- irritation leads to innovation.

**If mis-selling caused the first crisis, you would expect that everybody is focussing now on good-selling for a change? That we are all busy to turn cavemen into modern lovers?**

*You would expect so. But that is not the case.*

Most insiders will agree with my analysis. But I see that too many then forget about it. The issues get muddled and confused again, making it too complex for mere mortals to understand once again. Too many act as if the crisis was caused deep inside the snaking lines of domino-stones. Making it a game for insiders.

I am not disputing that these insider-games can do some good, but apart from some half-baked ethical oaths, the banking community does not focus on creating *good-selling* in a way that has real retail impact.

# The German meat-crisis.

### Is all of this something typical for banking?

*No. We have seen it in more retail-sectors. Like the German meat-crisis of some years ago.*

A bunch of shady German meat traders mixed in truck loads of slaughterhouse-rejects with loads of fresh meat. Remixed it, repackaged it, sold it on. The paper work of the good, fresh meat was stuck on these trucks. If you believed what was printed on the label, these crooks were trading in the *Triple-A* of meats. Nobody had an idea that there was a lot of rejected, potentially contaminated meat in there as well.

Nobody noticed, or nobody really cared, because nothing went really wrong. Some consumers may have had a bad stomach, or slight nausea, after consuming this meat. Then people got really ill. For vulnerable people the contaminated meat proved to do more than just upset a stomach.

The meat-scandal exploded.

### What happened to these German meat-traders?

*They were sent to jail. But the behaviour persists.*

From time to time new meat scandals pop up. It is too profitable. Legislation is planned to paint rejected meat from slaughterhouses a bright colour, to make it recognisable when repackaged.

If only we could do the same paint job with mortgages, Jon.

### Did these German meat-scandals topple the global meat-system?

*No, they didn't.*

These shady deals toppled the trust of the German public in meat for a while. But the shady practices of these meat-traders did not jeopardise the total German meat-sector. Let alone that this meat-scandal was felt world-wide.

Other food markets were not contaminated by the meat scandal. Not the bread market. The markets for vegetables felt no effect either. Nor the markets of fruit, milk or cheese. The negative effects were compartmentalised.

## But just a simple question then: why could the contaminated mortgage scandal poison the whole global system?

*Because mortgages consist of weightless bits & bytes. They travel fast.*

Information travels fast. Mortgages can circle the globe in seconds. Can be unpacked, cut up, remixed, repackaged, relabelled and resold repeatedly many times in the course of one day. World-wide.

Real meat travels slow. These meat guys had to truck heavy containers in the middle of the night from warehouse no.1 to warehouse no.2. Hire a crew to work in freezing conditions to physically unpack the meat, physically repack it, physically label it, put it in a new container, hire another truck, ship it to warehouse no.3. And so on, and so on.

In spite of all their determination, there were still thousands of European meat warehouses, where their contaminated meat didn't enter at all. That is why this and other food scandals didn't destroy the world-wide food chain. The Spanish oil, the Italian milk or the Austrian wine scandals, all the same story. Some had disastrous effects, some crossed borders, but none of them were able to contaminate all of our food systems worldwide.

## The need for re-inventing the retail model.
# Branches and trust.

Innovation in retail banking wasn't the hottest item on the agenda right after the crisis. In spite of the new found love that bankers have declared for safe and boring retail banking.

Banks are now stuck with eroded branches, all-time low customer trust and still too many bankers that didn't learn a thing from the crisis.

Retail bankers share their branches dilemma with porn-kings, record-stores, and travel agents:

"What to do with the damned branches... we can't do with them, we can't do without them... and they are getting costlier every week".

# Huge gap between internet and face-to-face banking.

**You keep on bashing the banks, but when it comes to our internet banking, the customers are extremely pleased with us.** *You're right, Jon. They should be.*

If we talk about direct banking the real and perceived added value has gone up tremendously. Costumers are very happy with that. We see here one of the few revolutions that has created a distinct win-win situation.

It brought you bankers immense cost-reductions, it brought the clients immense more value in many aspects.

Yes, transactional banking has adopted the tools and conventions of the IT-revolution to great effect. Now it's time to adopt the tools and conventions of the Information Retail Revolution to do the same in advisory and face-to-face banking.

Like porn-stores, record-stores and post-offices, bank branches must find a new function within the Information Retail Revolution media mix. Most banks haven't found that new function yet. Or worse, are not looking actively for it, apart from shutting them down.

# Re-inventing the branches.

**Okay, I work in retail banking. The branches are still giving me a headache. Am I the only one?**
*Every retail banking colleague of yours around the globe shares your headache.*

The branches are costing all of you a fortune. Yet, you can't do with them, you can't do without them. And you have the uneasy feeling that you are not doing a very good job in them. After the crisis, the necessary trust is certainly not rebuilt there.

**If we follow your thinking with the Information Retail Revolution, we do not need any branches in the future.**
*Not true. You'll need them for some time to come.*

You need face-to-face contact in the sales and advice process for some years to come. You have to reinvent the way you distribute that face-to-face contact from scratch, that's clear.

Locations that offer face-to-face support must be just one more access-point to your internet-driven main banking engine. And when we have a collection of those human advisors under one roof, then, yes, we have a bank-office, or indeed, a branch.

**But look at what is happening in porn and music, doesn't it mean that we should stop with all branches?**
*There are still a number of reasons to hang on to branches.*

Not just continuing with a pimped up version of what has been going on in bank-branches for the last decades, but a very focussed instrument within a multi-media strategy.

Here are some reasons why branches of a sort will be part of reality for some years to come.

*Physical distribution of money.*

Used to be the dominant reason for having branches; a real person handing out real money to another real person, who walks out with real cash.

That is still happening in large parts of the world, but it is dropping down at a great rate. No guessing why, as ATM's, shop-terminals, and internet banking take over.

We have come up with many solutions to make it drop down even quicker, but it's outside the scope of this book to go into detail on this issue.

*Physical intake of money.*

The mirror-image: the same consumer is now walking in with a wad of money in the bag, which she wants to put into her account.

Same declining rate of occurrence in most countries.

*Physical transfer of money.*

That can be to your grandmother who lives on the other side of the country, or it could be to pay a bill, but this habit is dying out rapidly too.

It is a market that is increasingly picked up by ordinary retail businesses in countries with many unbankables (=those not rich enough to own a bank account), as can be witnessed in developing countries.

*Physical distribution of secure mail.*

This is declining in most countries. When the nation's mail services cannot be trusted, or when people do not have addresses, a bank needs to get their cards, mail, contracts to the customer. Through their own channels. Your own couriers might do it too.

*Physical point in the sales-process.*

We can do much selling on the internet, but we still see that people go for the 'trustworthy-uncle' reassurance that a real person can give them.

Although that person-to-person advice can be given anywhere, an efficient form of distributing it is to put advisors in a building, to which the consumers can come. The same reason, why a supermarket is still a highly efficient concept. You make consumers do the travelling.

*Physical identification of persons.*

Electronic ID is going to be a feature in our not too distant future. But we are not there yet, and this development is at a different pace in different countries. We have found non-branch solutions for this too. *Physical evidence of your bank.*

Buildings with your name on it prove to the public that you exist. That makes sense, and we all know, that physical evidence declines, when you close a branch. Clients change bank when you close, even if they didn't visit your branch in the past three years.

Physical evidence is a reason why companies like Nike and Apple have huge flagship stores at high-traffic locations, like at Oxford Circus in London.

You may follow the same path, as we illustrated with iBank.

**Isn't it a bit easy to put the physical money flows outside the scope of this book? That is why we still have branches in many countries.**

*Separate these flows from sales and advice.*

That is how you should look into it. The old notion that you make your sales on the back of the physical money stream is just that: an old notion.

### Will reinventing my physical network cost me a fortune?

*Not at all. The main reinventing would be in software, which liberates costs in brick, mortar and people.*

You can increase the trust with your consumers multifold. Make gigantic reductions in the costs of your physical network at the same time. Without reducing your footprint.

On the contrary: you can increase your footprint considerably at the same time. And increase consumer satisfaction immensely.

## Cutting costs in branches.

**So, we will call the designers then?**

*No. First design the play. Only then can you design the props and the decor.*

Innovating branches by giving them a new paint-job doesn't help. It's sub-optimisation and as we heard in the same McKinsey study, such investments in unfocussed design are useless.

Innovations is not pouring drops of water on a hot plate. Drastic new thinking is necessary. Thinking outside of your sector helps here. Many radical but needed solutions can be found there.

## Eroded branches.

**The success of online banking has lead to an erosion of the perception of what goes on at our branches?**
*Most definitely. A typical Information Retail Revolution effect.*

While the price/value perception of online banking was rising quickly, the true and perceived price/value of face-to-face banking has dropped at the same rate.

You eroded the branches, without offering a bright new format instead. Things just got worse and worse. Discontinued branches, cutting off of direct phone contact to the branches, advisors pulled out of the branches, bad phone routines, which led to the usual call-centre irritation, etc. etc.

**Are the advisors less skilful today than they were in the past?**
*No. But in comparison they are.*

They lack the kind of tools that have become natural elsewhere in the Information Retail sectors. The way they have to work is getting more and more obsolete every day. And it shows. It's in contrast with the new Information Retail Revolution-routines that consumers are starting to expect. The internet makes the consumers smarter, which reduces the knowledge gap with advisors.

**Are these obsolete routines bad for the client?**
*Very much so.*

Advisors still have to offer verbal advice in a world where everybody has accepted audiovisual media as a standard. Audiovisual explanations? Most often what people get are hasty scribbles on the back of an envelope.

The client gets an advisor who has to diagnose off the top of his head, instead of with modern interactive Q&A decision tree models. That is why advisors tend to speak finance-technical abacadabra in the consumer's perception.

The advisors don't know the client. CRM systems? Non existent, or hopelessly outdated. Advisors lack even the most basic historic overview of the clients. At best they have to log in, log out between 6 or 7 systems. Which as a rule they don't do for lack of time.

Most products they are selling have a very low turnoverspeed, so it is hard to develop a routine. Personally matched product? Doubtful. Think Cavemen: the bosses of the advisor push him to sell the product-of-the-month. And do it fast.

Is it really surprising that the trust in the bank advisor is diminishing?

**Are the obsolete routines bad for us bankers? Or to put it more positively; would applying the Information Retail Revolution lessons make a difference for us?**

*A huge difference. You can have much more impact at much lower costs.*

The easiest quick-win lies in reducing these annoying sales-cycles that are the rule in even simple sales-processes. Go for instant satisfaction, and harvest that quick-win.

These sales-cycles exist due to lack of scenario's and advisory tools. They lead to low productivity of these expensive advisors. It results in network costs that are way too high compared with other Information Retail sectors.

Scattered data-grabbing means that data is still transferred from paper to computer, and manually transferred from one system to the next. Obsolete fulfillment procedures in the follow-up, after the sale has been made, are very costly and imprecise at best.

Obsolete routines lead to frustrated advisors, who see in other Information Retail sectors how it can be done better. Your advisors, Jon, live in the same age as their clients.

In order to manage the obsolete chaos, there are still too many costly management layers in place. Banks use far too expensive real estate on far too many square meters. With much too expensive interiors which are brought in as a fig-leaf for the absence of a strategy, but which lack even the most basic concept.

# Sales-cycles: bad for consumer, bad for bank.

### Can you describe how it works in many retail banks?

*Yes. I'll tell you the story of Marc and Vanessa.*

Marc is a 35 year old professional. Married to his working wife Vanessa, one kid. About to buy a house. That really nice house -sure it's expensive- but they both have a career that is going somewhere.

They have some money, so they would fall in what some banks call 'preferred' or 'premium' banking. One step *up* from average people's banking, one step *down* from private banking.

With that preferred banking deal they get their very own account manager, Ms. Smith. Marc and Vanessa decide to call her for a meeting.
*Phase 1: phoning to arrange a meeting*

Ms. Smith isn't available on the phone. Is that weird? Not at all. Statistically, the chance of Marc getting hold of Ms. Smith is close to zero. Let's do some calculating.

Two months of the year Ms. Smith is nowhere near the bank branch at all. Holidays, training, illness, pregnancy and the like.

In the other 10 months Ms. Smith is theoretically available for client contacts, but in reality is unavailable on the phone for most hours of the week.

She might be in a part-time job. But even if Ms. Smith is employed full time, the opening hours of the branch invariably exceed the amount of hours she is allowed to work. Disappointing for Marc and Vanessa, but there it is.

When Ms. Smith *is* in the branch, the reality is that most of the time Ms. Smith is not at her desk. She may be in a team meeting with her colleagues, having a smoke at the back door, or sorting out something for a client with a colleague.

And of course, the best explanation that Ms. Smith is not at her desk, is because she is in a meeting with a client.

In the few remaining hours per week that all of the above does not apply, Ms. Smith cannot be reached on the phone, because she is busy with phone calls.

This scenario is the rule in most banks that we know. Not the exception. It is a statistical certainty that in most cases Ms. Smith will not pick up the phone, but a colleague or the mailbox will do so.

With such a statistical certainty, you would expect that the bank has a clear phone protocol in place. That is very rare indeed. Unless you mean cutting off all phone access to local branches.

In the very best case, the colleague will stick a reminding post-it on Ms. Smith's computer screen. With name, phone-number, time and subject, if you're lucky. The harsh reality is that in many cases Marc's phone call will fall between the cracks.

The best banks can do is channel calls to a central call centre, which ordinarily doesn't do much good either, because they are not built with the consumer in mind. Recently we heard a phone engineer tell a regional manager of his bank: "You don't really want clients to phone their account manager, now do you?" Although he tried, the regional manager could not dissuade the engineer from this conviction.

Marc and Vanessa persisted, displaying a probably undeserved loyalty. After a couple of tries, they finally got hold of Ms. Smith and set up an appointment.

*The date of the meeting.*

In this age of instant satisfaction, chances are that the earliest available date is two or three weeks away. That is a lose-lose situation for everybody concerned.

Marc and Vanessa feel disappointed, stopped in their adrenalin-induced fever to arrange matters quickly.

For the bank it is very bad too. Any competitor that is quicker can intrude in the process, capturing Marc and Vanessa. Just because of the failure to deliver instant satisfaction.

*The meeting itself.*

Luckily no quicker competitor has intruded. Marc and Vanessa take half a day off. Simply because bank opening hours do not match their own non-working hours.

At the branch, they meet. A cold shower of a reception: 'Hello I'm Ms. Smith, before we start talking, can I make a photocopy of your passports?' Ms. Smith leaves Marc and Vanessa to stew in the meeting room while she takes care of the compliance issues.

Wasn't this an exploratory conversation, Marc and Vanessa wonder? Have we bought anything already? Why passports?

Ms. Smith returns and starts asking questions, to figure out if Marc and Vanessa can afford the desired amount. What she doesn't know is that they already did this test online. On the web-site of this very bank. They just want to know if they did it all right. But Ms. Smith has no access to their home page. She has to start all over again.

Then Ms. Smith will start the process to determine what type of mortgage will fit Marc and Vanessa best. This being their first house, Marc and Vanessa are quite insecure. They worry they won't comprehend financial technicalities. They are even more afraid to look stupid.

Choosing the right mortgage type is scary, because it affects the rest of your life. Or that is what Marc and Vanessa believe. They nurture a long term fear. They fear that making the wrong decision on a mortgage might eventually whip up their monthly payments into a huge financial wave that'll drown them.

Ms. Smith is happy to explain the differences. Verbally. To two nervous people that don't know the first thing about mortgages. The scribbles that Ms. Smith makes on that brand new sheet of white paper don't really explain matters in a soothing way either. They just add to the confusion. But both Marc and Vanessa are reluctant to ask too many stupid questions and pretend that they understand.

Ms. Smith may understand the technical aspects of the mortgages, but may also mistake the nervous nods of Marc and Vanessa for complete understanding. She has no tools to understand the precise repercussions of the decisions on the life of Marc and Vanessa.

That is why in many financial advice talks most clients at best only barely understand the options. At worst they don't understand it at all. In any case Marc and Vanessa hang on by their mental fingernails.

Their biggest fear is very short term. "When I leave the branch, will my fragile understanding shatter? Will these confusing issues slip through our fingers?" Ms. Smith promises Marc and Vanessa an envelope with a proposal in it. "Should be there in not more than a couple of weeks…"

Which makes Marc and Vanessa very nervous again. Ms. Smith is cutting them loose, and will confuse them with a letter, which most likely will be Chinese to them.

*The next step.*

Smith races to her next appointment, which will be a repetition of what she just did.

Sooner or later -she's busy.so it could be a couple of weeks- she'll find a moment to grab her notes from that morning with Marc and Vanessa.

Ms. Smith fiddles around with the different systems at her disposal. Logs in, logs out, logs in. It may take her 20 to 30 minutes to produce something rather off-the-peg. She struggles to comprehend her scribbles of the meeting that was one of many, and already some time ago. Personalising the offer and the cover letter would be too much to ask, she prints the offer and including a lot of legal papers, puts it in an envelope and sends it away to Marc and Vanessa.

*The offer arrives.*

Marc and Vanessa receive the long-awaited envelope. It feels heavy, and is thick. Somewhere deep into our evolutionary past we humans have developed a phobia for big envelopes. Chances are that this envelope ends up on the To-Do pile on the cabinet in the hall, next to the keys.

The reaction to such an envelope is always the same: an instantly shortened attention span, sweaty armpits, a heightened risk of skimming texts, instead of reading them, and a high likeliness to become distracted by anything remotely more entertaining, like repainting your entire house with a toothbrush. This may result in them not opening the envelope at all.

In case they do open it, Marc and Vanessa don't see the relationship between what they've been talking about three weeks earlier and the dancing words in front of them. Signatures required underneath incomprehensible small print scare them off. Most of it are mandatory legal stories. A lot of open questions confuse them. They will look at it later.

It'll take at least one more appointment before the open questions are answered. Before Marc and Vanessa are confident about the deal. Before the bank has made a sale.

# Incredible waste of productivity.

### Is this story of Marc and Vanessa not a bit over the top?

*Not really.*

I have personally witnessed this at many banks in many countries. This story has been checked with many bankers too. Ask around with bankers that you know; the Marc and Vanessa story is not untypical for a sales process in a bank.

It gets even more confusing when you realise that Marc and Vanessa run this obstacle course at one or two other banks as well.

### Sure it's long, and you juiced it up a bit, but the sale was made in the end, wasn't it? Where is the problem?

*Productivity. Out of a 100 of such cases, only 6,25 people make the deal.*

The other 93,75 wasted a lot of the valuable time of your front-line staff.

### Why do we end up with only 6,25 sales out of 100 prospects?

*Because of the inevitable drop out after each sales-cycle.*

A rule-of-thumb that we have developed over the years is that the drop-out rate of every sales-cycle is about 50%.

The average process may take about 5 steps. So you can make the calculations yourself: start with 100 people, lose 50, proceed with 50, then 25, then 12,5, and finally end up with 6,25 real sales.

### Reducing the number of sales-cycles can reduce waste, reduce costs and increase client satisfaction all at the same time?

*Precisely.*

Every sales-cycle that you reduce will double your productivity. And double your sales power and client satisfaction at the same time.

Putting instant satisfaction first, pays off great dividends. See how the lessons of the IRR can do so much good?

**There must be banks where all of what you describe above is not the case. Maybe ours is one?**

*Lucky you, Jon.*

There are indeed a few exceptions around the world. Just a few that have applied the learnings of the Information Retail Revolution. But they are still exceptions.

I will show them elsewhere in this book.

# Bankers' state of mind.

### What is the state of mind of retail bankers right now?

*Slowly waking up from the paralysis that the crisis imposed on them.*

During the last few years their banks have been concentrating on putting the toppled domino-stones back in place. With or without the aid of their governments. The resetting of the stones effort took all of their time and energy.

Retail banking has found a new sexiness. Most banks now voice a strong focus on retail banking due to its boring, unrisky and safe image. By the way; that's exactly why retail banking was so out of fashion before the crisis.

### Okay: a new belief in retail banking. But do the banks put their money where their retail mouth is?

*Not really. Very limited proof of that.*

Investments into new retail-thinking were halted directly after the crisis. A quite logical reaction, I agree. Those banks that had started to adopt the early learnings of the Information Retail Revolution also halted further innovation. A quite logical reaction too.

### Are there bankers that recognise the crisis as a fundamental call for retail innovation?

*Only a few define the crisis as more than a credit-crisis.*

Only a few have an inkling that banking is part of the Information Retail Revolution. Only very few feel the need to rethink their retail model from scratch.

Too many think like the video rental chains: "...just shutting down a few branches will be sufficient..."

Too many retail bankers are still convinced that there are no fundamental flaws in the way their retail model operates. Too many believe that it was just an unlucky financial crisis that made them topple over. That they weren't to blame anyway. Too many still believe that the concept of a universal bank is the most sound way to go forward.

## If retail banking is the new religion, we must be seeing many retail bankers leading the banks now?

*No. Investment bankers reign.*

Retail bankers never were the dominant species in the executive boards of banks. The alpha's, the most dominant types, tend to populate the upper floors of banks. Not retail bankers. Corporate bankers or investment bankers are alpha's.

Investment bankers are even more dominant. The alpha's of alpha's, indeed. Not surprising in view of the huge money-flows that were necessary to put the toppled domino-stones upright.

But you would at least expect that retail bankers would be asked to rethink their retail model in order to prevent the first stones to topple over again. But CEO-investment bankers tend to see reality through their perspective. They don't have the instinct to look at the first stones that fell. They feel that blocking risks further down the line will do the trick.

# The trust is gone.

### Isn't regaining consumer trust our main headache? Shutting branches will not do that?

*If you re-invent what the branches do, for whom at what time, they can restore trust in a big way.*

Already before the crisis the trust level of banks when compared to other retail sectors was atrocious. Because most bank advisors were forced to behave as cavemen in pinstripes, hitting the consumer on the head with the product of the month, instead of helping her with planning her financial life.

Consumer trust is lower than ever. Banks need to go a long way to win the hearts of customers again.

The crisis has shown that there are two very different types of trust. One of those trusts we had almost forgotten about. And with the other trust banks were not keeping up with other sectors. Let's look into them.

### What is trust-type no.1?

*The trust that you, the consumer, are dealing with a customer-centric company. That they have my interest in mind.*

On this type of trust banks were bypassed by other retail-sectors in the past decade.

With most large supermarkets chains in Europe or the US, Mrs. Consumer enjoys a deep-felt consumer-trust. The consumer believes that the chain is constantly researching what she needs, that they understand her, and what she wants. She also knows by experience that her supermarket acts on that knowledge.

She can find the latest products in her supermarket, in the varieties that she expects. Or didn't expect, but welcomed them as a pleasant and well-timed surprise.

She also has a trust that her supermarket chain offers the products at a *price* that she can afford. Because she trusts the market to keep these prices low, by the constant pressure of the competition.

Chains like Migros (Switzerland), Tesco (UK), Albert Heijn (Netherlands) or Carrefour (France) have built this trust for decades. Week in week out this promise of trust was confirmed. Time and time again.

This consistent consumer-orientation translates into immense trust-figures; Swiss consumers believe that Migros is -by far- the most trusted brand in the country.

Way above the trust the Swiss consumer allocates to banks.

### Trust no.2?

*The trust that the products are safe. That they are not dangerous.*

She expects that the meat at her supermarket is not contaminated with evil viruses, that the milk isn't sour, the eggs not infected with salmonella, that the wine doesn't contain anti-freeze. When Mrs. Consumer shops at Migros, Tesco, Albert Heijn or Carrefour, she has a built-in trust that the products she buys will not harm her or her family.

### How do banks stand in these trust-issues?

*Shamefully low in both types.*

While supermarkets gained more and more trust over the last decades, banks didn't grow theirs at the same rate which resulted in an increasing gap of trust between the sectors.

But in spite of all that, at least your money was safe with your bank. Banks were generally regarded as not being consumer-oriented the way supermarkets were, but the banks were not threatening the financial health of you and your family.

It is this second type of trust that has shattered, once the domino-stones of the crisis started to fall.

**But there were some banks who did well. Were the stones didn't topple. Did these banks not get all of the market?**

*No. The rescue operations of the government prevented the market to clean out bad performers.*

There were a few weeks early in the crisis, when uncontaminated, reliable banks were seen as the preferred place to send your money to. State-owned Postbanks had a brief stretch of luck, because of the suddenly advantageous effects of their boring, dull, state-owned image.

But the market, which stimulates supermarkets to be consumer-oriented, was prevented to clean up the dirty acts of the under-performers. The market did not force them to become consumer oriented. They weren't forced to solve the core-problem: preventing the first stones to topple. The market didn't reward good-selling, it accepted mis-selling to continue unopposed.

# Responsibility of the consumer?
# Or the bank?

**Isn't there the responsibility of the consumer too? They are grown-ups, aren't they? Shouldn't they look after their own affairs?**

*Hey, Jon, would you expect the same attitude from your supermarket, your doctor or your pilot?*

Do you check whether the pills the doctor prescribes you might have a negative effect in 5 years time? Or do you rely on his wisdom and experience? Don't you have a built-in trust that -first and foremost- he will take your long-term interest at heart?

Do you check with the pilot of your plane, whether he has taken enough fuel onboard, so it will lasts the whole flight, even when he has to take a longer route, because of possible thunderstorms?

**Do supermarkets believe that it is the responsibility of the consumer to check the meat, eggs or milk for potential health-threats to her and her family?**

*Of course not.*

Mrs. Consumer doesn't check the meat herself. She doesn't open the wine to check for anti-freeze traces. She doesn't carry an analysis set for eggs. In most big supermarket chains in developed countries, Mrs. Consumer doesn't think twice about this core-trust; the products are safe. She leaves the checking to the supermarket. Trusts the competition between supermarkets to keep the pressure on. And in the back of her mind she knows that there is a government institution that checks her health issues for her.

In case something goes wrong she expects the supermarket chain to have an immediate and widely-publicised call-back. Which prevents the spreading of the problems. Much more trustworthy than the banks do it, eh?

**But banking clients can act very irresponsibly, can't they? In spite of everything they sometimes choose to take a too large loan, which may be hazardous in the long term.**
*Did you make that very clear to them?*

Did you make a financial x-ray? Did you make sure? Did you have a good picture of their financial history? Enough to verify that they are taking the right product? Honestly?

**Easy to say, but such an attitude of advising like a doctor would cost us lots of business. The stubborn customer can go to one of our competitors and get that not-so-healthy mortgage anyway...**
*Stop calling yourself advisors then.*

What should be on your business-card? Bank advisor? Or bank salesmen? Make up your mind. What is the difference then between having an advisor and an execution-only relationship? What is your advice worth, if you do not prevent your customers from making far-reaching mistakes?

# Put some blame on the consumers too, please.

**You put the blame a bit too much on the banks. Put some on the consumers too, please. Don't you forget that legions of over-excited consumers pulled the credits out of the hands of credit-salesmen and bank-advisors? That they had a great party on all that credit? And -not unimportant- that this credit-craze did the economy a world of good as well?**

*Agreed, Jon. But don't we accept protection against unhealthy temptations in most other areas of life?*

We all may be tempted to do very nice, but very unhealthy things from time to time, don't we? To drive just a few miles too fast? To drink a tiny bit too much while driving? To ask our doctor for nice but quite unnecessary pills?

We accept that there are rules in place that protect us against our unhealthy temptations, don't we?

We all accept that the doctor has the duty to tell his patients to forget those nice, yet unnecessary pills? Don't you feel that it's a good thing that the doctor can tell you so, with the confidence that the doctor a few doors down the road will deny you those nice & unhealthy pills as well?

**Could we have stayed out of the market when all other bankers were throwing a wild and very profitable party?**

*Wild indeed. But profitable? In hindsight?*

Shouldn't we deduct the costs of the crisis from the profit-party of those wild years? Did those mortgages show a profit then? Of course not, Jon.

**Did some banks stay out of the wild credit party?**

*Yes. Some did.*

I know a bank that is active in middle-Europe. Let's call it Bank X. This Bank X refused to issue mortgages in Swiss Francs and other hard currencies, at a time when that was high fashion, and many other banks made a bundle with them.

The other banks probably described Bank X as a bunch of sissies then. History proved Bank X very right indeed.

## Just clarify for me: what was this hard-currency mortgage scandal?

*A sector-wide case of highly irresponsible mis-selling.*

In a number of middle European countries, all outside the euro-zone, mortgages in hard currencies were marketed extensively. It was cheaper. Hungary is a good example. You would pay 6 or 7% interest when the loan was in Swiss francs, but 13 or 14%, if you took the loan in the far less sexy Hungarian Forint.

But somewhere, hidden inside those nice mortgages and loans, a time-bomb was ticking away, of course. Waiting for the moment that the value of the weak Forint versus the strong Swiss Franc would drop. Which eventually it did.

The currency-time-bomb exploded, and many, many people and companies in those countries were hurt badly. It toppled banks, but worse, it toppled the crisis-hit central European economies in its wake.

That's when domino stones toppled further, hitting fashions chains and supermarkets too. They all experienced a sector-wide massive drop in turnover. A quarter or more of their turnover just melted away. Simply because the majority of the Hungarian households was strangled by their suddenly very unsexy Swiss loans.

That effect is felt right up to now: supermarket chiefs in those markets look closely at the exchange rate; a further drop of the Forint or Krone makes the Swiss loans eat up even more of the disposable household incomes. That translates in immediate drops in the monthly turnover in their stores.

See how how far the toppling domino's of mortgages can reach? A perfect example of the far reaching effects of mis-selling, I would think.

**It makes sense then to put the consumer's interest first?**
*It does.*

We have been talking about *life-time client value* a lot in the banking sector, Jon. The concept is valuable. Change your values and your tools accordingly. In the next chapter I will describe one of the champions of consumer-centric retailing.

**Selling kitchens is like selling financials.**

# How would Ikea do banking?

Ikea from Sweden has revolutionized furniture retailing in the past decades. They have liberated Mrs. Consumer from the claws of pushy, bonus-driven salesmen in shady furniture stores.

One sector still escaped their consumer-centric approach: kitchens, one of the largest and scary decisions in any household. Until recently it was assumed that you could not sell a kitchen without knowledgable advice from salesmen.

Ikea turned that conventional wisdom on its head. With great success. And with many parallels with the financial sector.

# Ikea could sell financials even better.

**There is talk about supermarket banking. Would they be the only retailers in financial services?**
*Ikea can do it just as well, and probably even better.*

Ikea's excellent value for money proposition and natural consumer focus will transfer easily and effectively to financial services. The Ikea Family Card has a payment facility on it in several countries. They can extend that financial relationship with confidence. Step by step, just as Marks & Spencer did it in the UK. And Ikea can roll out the concept worldwide in a way no bank can.

Last but not least: Ikea is very experienced at extending their strong brand values into new categories. As we have witnessed with their restaurants, supermarkets, kitchens and even *houses*. Yes, indeed, Ikea could do serious damage to the banking world.

# Ikea and heavy financial products.

**But Ikea is about simple do-it-yourself furniture. They cannot compete in our banking market, which depends largely on face-to-face advice?**

*They conquered the far more complex kitchen market, didn't they?*

Ikea pioneered a complete new approach in a sector that was once dominated by old-fashioned retail-concepts which relied heavily on conventional *face-to-face salesmen* for success and market share.

**But Ikea will never grab serious market-share in the heavier financial products like mortgages or pensions.**

*Don't count on it.*

Ikea grabbed very serious market-share from the *salesmen driven* kitchen retailers within one decade. I learned in a recent Sunday Telegraph interview with Ikea CEO, Mikael Ohlsson how much market share:

"We have a big focus on kitchens now. We have developed that over the past decade. Every second kitchen in Norway is Ikea, every third in Sweden, every third in France..."

**The kitchen-sector wasn't as dependent on face-to-face advice as banks are today, was it?**

*Wrong. It was the only way to go. Until Ikea.*

The kitchen-retail sector has always been convinced that without *face-to-face* salesmen you could forget it. They believed that there was no other way to help the consumer through that very complex and scary process of planning, designing and buying your kitchen.

And scary it is: a new kitchen eats a big chunk out of your family budget, has long-term consequences if you get it wrong, and is something you only need a few times in your life. That made the whole process dazzlingly complex and created the ideal combustible environment for an explosive row with your wife.

By surrendering yourself to a kitchen salesman you hoped to ease that scary feeling somewhat, but you *knew* you had entered a very asymmetric relationship at the same time. Your salesman had access to much more information than you. He knew how to get all the confusing different elements of the kitchen together into one comprehensive plan. And last but not least, he, and his competitors, kept the price-setting shady and intransparent. On purpose. On top of that: he pushed you, wanted to close the sale, as he was driven by bonuses.

To make it worse: you knew you had to go through the whole terrible and scary process at a couple of other kitchen-specialists too. If only to get quotes. For complex products and services that were impossible for you to compare. And each time you knew you were negotiating against an unequal opponent. Leaving you with the sinking feeling that you would pay far too much in any case.

The kitchen salesman *never* was your advisor. Never your 'trustworthy uncle'. He was a salesman first and foremost. Conflicting emotions? Yes, indeed. Do you feel the painful knot in your neck coming on, when I tell this story? Yes? A bit like going to your mortgage advisor?

That was indeed true for a long time. Until Ikea changed things.

# Ikea took the 'scary' out of it.

**Can Ikea supply the 'trustworthy uncle' function better than salesmen-driven kitchen-retailers? Or banks for that matter?**

*Yes, indeed. They revolutionised it and took the 'scary' out of the product, the process and the price.*

They have done everything to take as much complexity out of the relationship as possible. Making the relationship as symmetrical as possible. As modern lovers do. By opening up everything to the consumer. By giving you control. Taking away inequality. Offering the security that at the end of the process you will have -guaranteed- the best price in the market. Without nerve-racking bargaining, plus a *no-questions-asked* money back guarantee.

They took the complexity out of the products in the usual Ikea-way. By taking the confusion out of the assortment, components and options. One set of technical components which you can personalise and differentiate as much as you like. They created great planning and highly visual designing software too. Which you can access and re-access time and again. Work through in one IT-flow. At home, in the store, back home again. Because it is the one and the same IT platform you're working on. They re-engineered their planning and advice processes to become pretty uncomplex.

But still, Ikea knows a certain level of complexity is unavoidable in planning a kitchen. You still will feel nervous and scary moments: *"...have I done it well so far?"* You need human help and -especially- reassurance along the way. Ikea took care of that too: they reengineered *face-to-face* advice procedures to fill those gaps that can only be filled by human support. They created and choreographed 'trustworthy uncles', or better: 'trustworthy *cousins*'. Created the tools which makes them effective. Made them really trustworthy too, because the Ikea kitchen advisors are not bonus-driven salesmen in disguise, but just advisors. Not with a university degree, but just shop-assistants with some training and software. They are just there to help you *buy*. Not to *sell*. Your relationship is not personal with one person. You have a relation with the Ikea *system*, in which advisors play their predetermined and limited role.

Ikea has deconstructed and reconstructed the process from the ground up. (Not unlike our PPMMC way, which I write about elsewhere in this book.) That's how they have taken away the asymmetric aspect out of the process. You don't need the warm hand of your personal individual advisor anymore. You no longer feel any pressure in the process. Gone is the nervous and suspicious feeling you had.

**The Ikea kitchen process is how you would like us bankers to reengineer our retail formats?**
*Exactly.*

Within 10 years Ikea have simplified not only the concept of kitchen products but all the advisory and delivery processes too. That way they have reduced the costs in the usual dramatic Ikea way. Which allows them to offer very low prices for a great kitchen and a great process. Which explains their unbeatable NoCompromise position.

Wouldn't your customers like that from your bank, Jon?

# Ikea does it with a few stores.

### What else can we bankers learn from Ikea?

*That you don't need many stores to cater for high-value, low-frequency consumer needs.*

People are prepared to drive for their large household investments. Especially when the destination is special and offers the security of NoCompromise: high value at low prices.

There are only 6 Ikea stores in Norway. That is 1 store per 460 thousand Norwegians. With just these stores half of the kitchens sold in Norway are now Ikea-kitchens, if we believe Mikael, the CEO, in that Sunday Telegraph interview. In Sweden each of the 17 Ikea stores has to cater for 530 thousand Swedes, and now every third kitchen sold in a Swedish home is Ikea. In France they do an even more impressive job. Not more than 28 Ikea stores in France have sold every third French kitchen. Mind you; that calculates to 1 store per 2,2 *million* Frenchmen.

That's a tempting future for your brick & mortar, isn't it Jon?

### But people prefer to do business with someone they have a relationship with? Close by, with a face they trust? Like us banks?

*No, they don't.*

If I type in *kitchen* on the Stockholm Yellow Pages I get almost 1,500 returns. Ikea has just 2 stores there. And still sells 1 out of 3 kitchens.

Be real: how much of a relationship can you build with your kitchen salesman? How many times in your life do you change your kitchen anyway? Is the same salesman that sold your last kitchen still working there? Or if he is, would you remember him? Is there really a relationship?

Isn't the same true for banking? Can you honestly say most of your retail banking clients have a relationship with you? They don't, Jon. That would be an unrealistic claim.

**But I cannot close almost all my bank-branches! I cannot survive with just a handful with each one catering for 500 thousand citizens. Let alone 2,2 million!**

*Get used to the idea, Jon. And create a paradigm shift.*

Learn from Ikea that their stores are not just a larger, pumped-up version of those terrible old-fashioned kitchen-stores. No, Jon. They haven't scaled up the usual salesman-centric approach. You are not attacked at the Ikea front door by hundreds of pushy salesmen. Instead Ikea re-invented the entire business model of the sector, and proved all these old-fashioned thinkers entirely wrong.

Invent something completely new and NoCompromise there, Jon. An exciting, fully integrated visit to your internet-driven channel.

# Ikea is the same world-wide.

**Interesting, Hans, but such thinking will not be right for my country. Banking is so different from country to country.**
*Ikea has 1 concept in 316 stores in 38 countries all around the world.*

All follow the same format, the same concepts. I know, I have visited them in many countries. Sure, in Sweden Ikea will sell less garden furniture in the winter than they will do in Spain. But the Ikea principles stay exactly the same everywhere.

If Ikea is able to achieve such impressive market shares with one concept in all these countries in something as highly personal as your home, don't tell me that such thinking would be impossible in banking.

**If Ikea were to enter banking, would they be a threat to us banks?**
*Oh, yeah! Most certainly.*

The moment they apply their conceptual thinking to financial services there won't be much stopping them. They will achieve impressive market shares with their proven consumer-focus. What may stop them would be whether they will bring the necessary commitment and whether they are capable of integrating financial services in their corporate culture.

**What to do now?**
*Don't wait for it to happen, Jon.*

Stop wasting your breath on down-playing this indisputable threat. Start re-inventing your business from scratch by learning from *their* lessons.

## From caveman to modern lover.
# Modern match-making.

Banks should put all effort in the matching process which comes before the actual sale of the product. It's where most impact can be made. It is where most things went wrong. It is where most costs in today's banking are coming from.

# Modern romance brings productivity.

### How can we transform our cavemen in pinstripes into modern lovers?

*Apply the new tools of the Information Retail Revolution.*

New media can help transform cavemen into modern lovers. On top of that: it's how you can cut the cost of your branch network by some 25-50%.

### But is Mrs. Consumer ready for a bank advisor who advises with the help of his computer screen?

*The Information Retail Revolution has made it her new standard.*

The consumer expects it. And expects it everywhere. What the consumer finds natural in the way he or she obtains music, travel, jobs, will also be natural in her banking needs.

Bankers have the tendency to think within their own sector. That is only human, it is what music-executives do as well. The consumer, though, doesn't feel restricted by the boundaries of a sector.

She perceives new media, new applications, new ways of interacting, new ways of customising in one sector, and transfers them to other sectors without a second thought. With every new sector she transfers these new conventions to, the conventions become more expected.

Trying to make bankers behave like modern romantic lovers with sales training or -even more of a joke- a code of ethics will not force the change. New Information Retail Revolution-tools will.

### What was the incentive before the crisis to make these bankers stop with their caveman concept of romance?

*Immensely higher levels of productivity.*

Creating a more modern, listening, mutually beneficial type of relationship can lead to much, much higher levels of productivity. I have calculated at various banks that it could reduce your branches-costs by 25% to 75%.

That's quite exciting in itself, isn't it?

## What should be the incentive now, after the crisis?

*All of the above. Plus, as nice added benefit: prevent crisis no.2.*

Preventing the first domino-stones from toppling over brings a huge, immeasurable gain. To consumers. To banks. To society.

That is made even more tangible when you get the benefits of much higher productivity too.

## When you told bankers this story did they all run back to their companies and start to put things right?

*That's rare.*

Solving the front-line problems of mis-matching, or even worse, non-matching, invariably gives way to more pressing issues.

That was the case before the crisis, that is still the case.

Other priorities are invariably higher. And, well to be honest, stopping the worst collapses in the financial systems did have some priority in the past two to three years.

# How healthcare matches the right pill to the right person.

**You talk about unhealthy effects of heady products. Isn't that like healthcare?**

*Precisely.*

Many pharmaceuticals are dangerous, even poisonous, when you and I consume them at will. Even simple aspirins can be very dangerous if you swallow too many of them.

But for some people even the most risky medicines are very, very beneficial. Even in very high doses that would make you and me very ill indeed.

Ask any cancer-patient.

**So the medical world puts a lot of effort in sophisticated matching-processes?**

*It is the core-business of a doctor.*

We all know how much time is invested in developing his diagnosis and therapy skills. How much time is put into creating your medical history. How much time is invested in building well-tuned teams of specialists to help the doctor with his diagnosis.

How much effort is put into the most advanced diagnosis instruments? How much money is spent on intricate diagnosis software? How careful is the medical world in grabbing and storing all kinds of data on you?

**Do you consider a doctor to be an example for the InformationRetail sector?**

*Very much so. In fact they are a part of it.*

A doctor is as much a part of the InformationRetail sector as an intermediary at a temp agency, or a travel agent. They all are matching their skills to the needs of the client.

**Well, eh, to be honest..., the diagnosis-bit, the matching process at most banks is incomparable with that of doctors, isn't it?**
*That's an understatement.*

Do we have the financial equivalent of X-rays? Financial MRI-scans? If only! Isn't the diagnosis-process in retail banking not shamefully insufficient by comparison? Do banks think from the consumer inwards? Or from the product outwards?

That is my main argument: stop selling, start matching. That will turn mis-selling into good-selling. Isn't that what we should do in retail banking?

**Too much praise for the medical world: I can tell you some horror stories about doctors and pharmaceutical companies!**
*Sure you can.*

The stories about bad apples don't hide the fact that the medical profession as such is focussed on putting the long-term interest of the patients as the main priority.

# While you were busy cleaning up after the crisis.

### So you feel that we in banking should be more serious about thinking up new retail formats?

*Yes. The Information Retail Revolution did not stop while you were cleaning up the mess of the crisis. Get on board now, Jon.*

The Information Retail Revolution grew and grew, Jon. Many retail sectors were infected. The crisis accelerated that growth. Now you are slowly getting out of the immediate emergency phase of the crisis, the phase of putting all the domino-stones back up. A couple of years have passed now. In that time you didn't really do much about re-engineering your retail formats. Now that you have the time to start looking around again, you'll find that the Information Retail Revolution has exploded from infancy into full maturity, Jon.

The same dynamics of the Information Retail Revolution that is so *threatening* to you, Jon, is giving you loads of *opportunities* at the same time. It is offering you the unique chance of making your bank really consumer-focussed. At much lower costs. But in order to do some serious innovation, we need to discuss some serious irritation.

### Are we in for a round of unrestricted bank-bashing here, Hans?

*No, Jon. But only a clean analysis of what went wrong can lead to how we can make it right.*

The whole world knows what caused the crisis, but that analysis gets so muddled up in the confusion since then, that the sector fails to keep its focus on where it all started. If that analysis irritates a bit Jon, I understand, but you know the old saying: *only irritation can cause innovation.* And there is enough innovation in this book.

## Learn from Information Retailers.

# IRR rules that would do banks a world of good.

Many lessons from other Information Retail sectors can be applied to retail banking.

It will make your bank go from mis-selling to good-selling. The Information Retail Revolution makes this possible on a massive scale at low cost.

Use the lessons from the Information Retail Revolution lessons to help you prevent crisis no.2.

# Information Retail Revolution Rules.

**You are talking about good-selling. All very fine, but how can we do that on the large scale of our bank, and not be drowned by the costs?**

*By applying the new Information Retail Revolution Rules.*

The Information Retail Revolution teaches us lessons. Some are already well-developed. Others are in the process of developing. We can learn from them. Let's try to understand some of these Information Retail Revolution Rules. If only out of defensive reasons; the winners of tomorrow will use them. But why not out of offensive reasons too. If they can use these rules, so can you, Jon.

Before anything else: accept that you are part of the information retail sector. Then rethink your business models from scratch. And become the winner.

**Are the rules of the Information Retail Revolution really ground-breaking?**

*Surprisingly, many of them have been around for ages. But their speed of development is new.*

Some of the deciding Information Retail Revolution Rules are age-old retail wisdom, like Consumer Passion, Retail is Detail, Transparent Assortment. In the Information Retail Revolution times you can give new meaning to these rules.

Other Information Retail Revolution Rules are new. Customising, MyPrefs, and Genius are new tricks. They would be impossible without IT. All of them rapidly became widely accepted conventions. They can easily be adopted by banking. Or even stronger: *should* be adopted, because people expect it. From music-retailers, travel agents, porn-kings. And banks.

# No Compromise is the main trend.

### What is the most important rule, the main overriding trend?
*Think NoCompromise.*

Mrs. Consumer does not accept compromises in value, or compromises in price anymore. She wants it here. She want it now. She wants it cheap. Or -if possible- for free. Good for her: plenty of companies offer that NoCompromise to her. Those who don't, are left behind more and more.

### What exactly is NoCompromise?
*Look at this basic positioning model.*

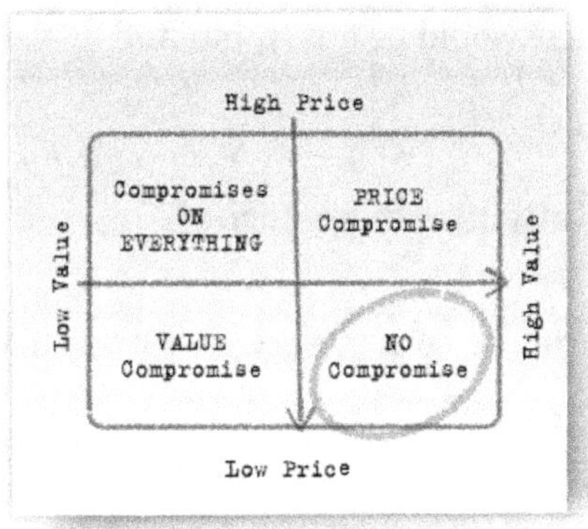


*The NoCompromise Positioning Model, seen from the perception of Mrs. Consumer.*

Positioning is no rocket science. Mrs. Consumer plots your position in this simple and age-old diagram. She plots Value on one axis, Price on the other. She would love it if she could do business with you in the NoCompromise corner; where she would get Low Price and High Value at the same time.

**But we can't give her both High Value as well as LowPrice, can we? The costs would ruin our earning model.**

*That's old fashioned thinking.*

It's what you learned at business school, didn't you? Michael Porter told you that Mrs. Consumer can't have it both ways. Sorry, but life sucks, Michael told us: Mrs. Consumer *must* make an unwelcome choice. She can pick High Value. Alas, that will mean she has to accept the compromise of High Price. She can pick Low Price. But alas again, she has to accept the compromise of Low Value. She can't pick both, is what Michael told us.

Conventional thinking dictates that no company can survive in the NoCompromise corner. The cost of offering High Value to Mrs. Consumer would demand such High Costs, that you would be forced to charge High Prices.

Sorry, Mrs. Consumer, NoCompromise would be lovely, but not possible.

**So can companies survive in the NoCompromise corner?**

*New players change the rules.*

Many companies in the Value Compromise corner every year start on a challenging journey. There goal is the NoCompromise corner. Just a few succeed on that journey, most fail. In spite of all their good intentions most find out that raising Value raises Costs. Which in turn raises Prices. Before you know you have ended up in the PriceCompromise corner. Or worse; in the middle of the diagram; offering unappetising Medium Value at unappetising Medium Prices.

The few that succeed to keep Costs low on this journey, ultimately become NoCompromise retailers. At first they are small, and neglected by the old players. A few will grow and grow and grow. The consumer loves them. Obviously. What can beat High Value at Low Prices?

Think of H&M and Ikea from Sweden, Kaufland from Germany, Tesco from the UK, Walmart in the USA, Google, Amazon and iTunes to name a few. They all have achieved to make a successful journey towards the NoCompromise corner.

## What determines Value? What determines Price?

*That's up to Mrs. Consumer.*

It's her perception that counts. What defines Value to her is more mundane than industry-insiders want to admit; location, accessibility, getting a returning phone call, raises value more than the latest financial wiz-kid product.

She gets more and more impatient as well. Whoever satisfies her needs the quickest is rated as the highest value in today's markets. Good for her: the Information Retail Revolution caters for that need.

What determines Price? That is also defined by *her* perception. What we invariably see is that it's more about price-*trust* than mathematically researched real price differences.

# NoCompromise players cause a paradigm shift.

### Why can NoCompromise retailers topple the old players?

*They cause a paradigm shift.*

Mrs. Consumer readily embraces the new definitions of HighValue and LowPrice that the NoCompromise player establishes. She makes these her new standard, her new benchmark. The moment that the new NoCompromise competitors have built up enough mass, they will cause a paradigm shift. The market forces will be redefined. Forever. She will expect from *everybody* the new NoCompromise definitions. That's when the total playing field starts to move South East.

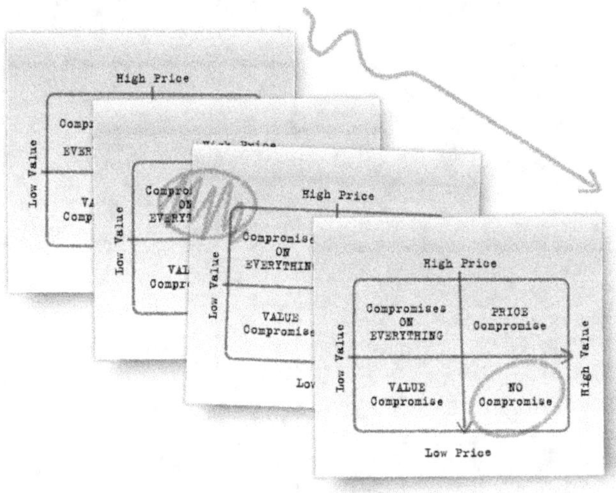


*The playing field shifts South East in time, leaving old players outside the field.*

## But if the market shifts position, everybody will follow!

*Most don't. They don't recognise the threat, or if they do, it's often too late.*

The new inhabitants of the NoCompromise corner are small at first. They don't have enough mass yet to shift the playing field. When they build up mass gradually, the playing field starts to shift a little. The first minuscule shifts are not felt by the old players. They don't recognise it, or when they do, they downplay it. The new NoCompromise players play by different rules; they are not seen as a direct threat: "They can never survive in the NoCompromise corner. We've tried, and it can't be done."

Then the playing field starts to move SouthEast with more speed. The old players do not perceive this as a market-defining trend, but downplay it as a temporary bad spot. That is the moment when they might have had enough time to adapt and move with it. But invariably old players fail to recognise the move before it's too late. Their powerful position over decades has made them short-sighted and arrogant. They waste valuable time downplaying the threat. And when they finally recognise the market is really shifting, they engage in internal and paralysing quarrelling.

Recognise it, Jon?

In the end the old players can't develop the necessary agility or speed and get left behind. Forever. Before you know it, they end up in the *Compromises On Everything* corner. Or are left in the cold, and off the playing field all together. Which is just one step away from total extinction.

Nothing stays still in the economy, Jon. There will always be a new competitor who outperforms the old NoCompromise player on value, or price, or both. It's Darwinistic capitalism, whether you like it or not.

# IRR gives the NoCompromise shifts turbo-power.

### What does the Information Retail Revolution change in this eternal NoCompromise evolution?

*The NoCompromise playing field shifts position with turbo-speed.*

The NoCompromise playing field has always moved to the South East. In the Information Retail Revolution the incredible *speed, with which the playing field moves,* is new.

Values are re-defined. In a few years. A few months. Overnight. Old values become obsolete and utterly unattractive. Overnight. Prices are decimated at the same incredible speed. Why pay anything at all? Who can beat free? The Information Retail Revolution gives the NoCompromise shifts turbo-speed.

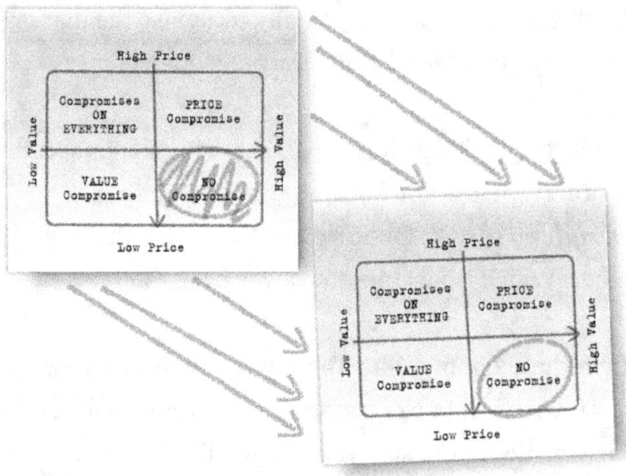


*The Information Retail Revolution makes the playing field move at turbo-speed, not allowing for gradual steps in between.*

**Some examples of the new speed of the NoCompromise shifts?**

*Take MySpace or video rentals.*

MySpace was the ultimate NoCompromise player for sharing music and video. Murdoch bought this hit-company for more than 500 million dollars 5 years ago, and started to make it unbearably slow and heavy with old-school earning instruments. Facebook and YouTube developed new, athletic, free interaction, bypassed MySpace, and are the new NoCompromise players. MySpace has been left behind in the CompromisesOnEverything corner. Which, as we know now, is one step away from extinction.

One more, even more fast-moving example. The Dutch market of video rentals dropped 40% (!) within half a year in 2010. New download possibilities and cable television offered instant satisfaction at rock bottom prices or free. The NoCompromise playing field moved South East with incredible speed. Exit the video rentals, the big players went bankrupt.

# Banking doesn't live on an island.

### Okay, the Information Retail Revolution might make the playing field move, but does that hit banking?

*Banking doesn't live on an island, you are part of Information Retail.*

The Information Retail Revolution redefines standards. One retail sector after another followed. That is causing a paradigm shift in banking too. The expected standards and prices in information products and services are fundamentally redefined by all those retail sectors that offer the new NoCompromise of the Information Retail Revolution. The advice and sales activities of the banking sector have been left behind in an utterly unpromising Compromises On Everything corner, way outside the main playing fields.

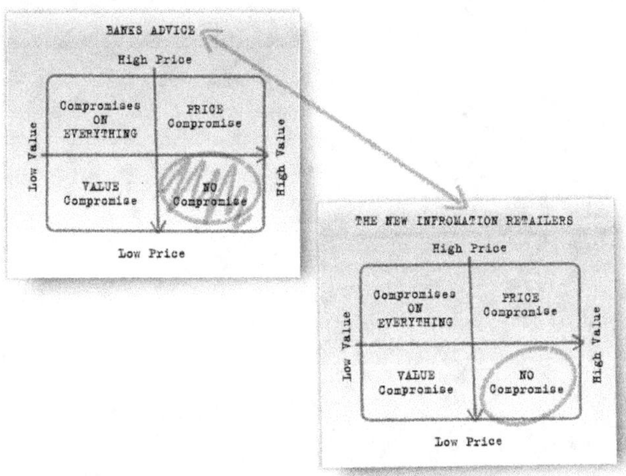


*The bank sector is left behind, when compared to other Information Retailers.*

When it comes to face-to-face banking, you are way outside the playing field. Once the NoCompromise players in financial services have created enough mass, you'll slide off it even further. We know what happens then: end-of-lifetime troubles erupt, management is renewed at ever-increasing speed, valuable time is lost with internal guerilla warfare.

Don't kid yourself, Jon, it can happen to mighty large companies like banks too.

Look at how the once-mighty mass market department stores have toppled in the past decades. Slowly but surely new competitors on both value and price nibbled away at their position. Slow decision processes in these 100-year old companies made it impossible to look reality in the face, let alone adapt to the changing position of the playing field. Today most of them are bankrupt, leaving ugly holes in inner-city retail areas.

Getting bypassed by moving markets is nothing new; it is the eternal Darwinian law of economic life. It can happen to banks too.

# Banks are split into two positions.

### Where would you position banks?

*1. In the very desirable NoCompromises corner.*

Internet banking, mobile phone banking, ATM's, paying with your card in a store, etc... Transactional banking has adopted the Information Retail Revolution tools with great elegance. It's made life nicer for bank clients in many countries.

*2. Way off the playing field.*

The other side of banking, the one where personal contacts are needed, is in deep shit. You offer a lousy service at a high price. This is not a sustainable concept: Mrs. Consumer hates you for it. She will escape from you, the instant she has an alternative. From what we have seen in the other Information Retail Revolution sectors, new alternatives are forming everywhere.

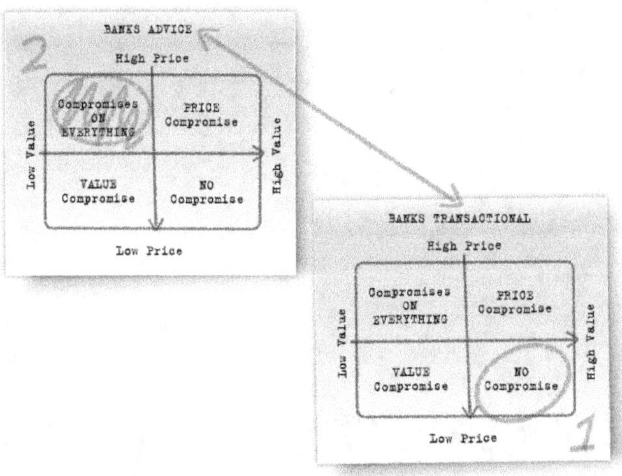


*Two very separate positions for banks in most countries.*

**We can't be way off the playing field and still survive. The market would force us out of business, wouldn't it?**

*Which market, Jon?*

Yes, I agree, in free markets companies can not survive long when they are so far off the playing field.

The only companies that can survive there are monopolists. Or oligopolists, when a handful of large firms call the shots in a market. Or companies that are protected by government, corruption or crime.

Monopolists, oligopolists and protected companies are safe from the storms of the markets, because the free market mechanism is kept outside the door.

**How would you explain the survival of banks when they are so far off the playing field?**

*Banks are government-protected oligopolists in many cases.*

The banking sector was pretty much a closed shop before the crisis. The same neglect of consumers and retail banking could be found at every bank. A oligopoly, a shared neglect of consumer-focus.

There wasn't much real choice for Mrs. Consumer, or Mr. Businessman. Changing banks wasn't rewarding. An old Dutch proverb explains it well: "…it doesn't really matter whether you are bitten by the cat or the dog…"

After the crisis it didn't get much better. Governments pumped in shit-loads of money to prevent banks toppling over, which put a stop to any cleansing effect that the natural forces of the free market might have had.

# Towards NoCompromise: the Value-makers.

**I take up the challenge, Hans. I want to become the NoCompromise bank of the Information Retail Revolution. How do I do that?**

*Apply the Information Retail Revolution **Values** first, Jon.*

In the following pages I have made a selection of values that will have the most impact. They will make your bank shift to the right.

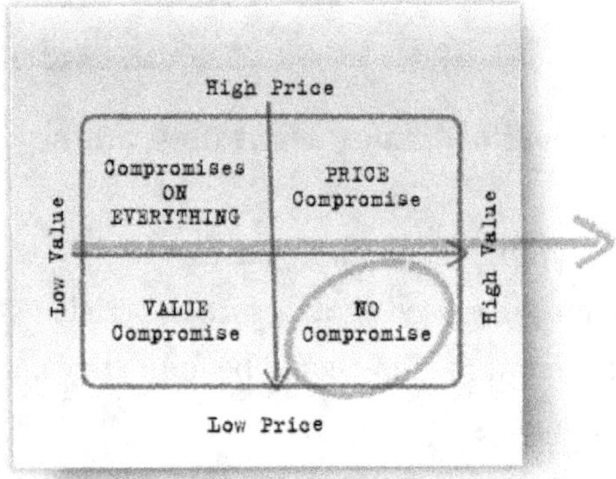


*Towards NoCompromise. The Value-elements of the Information Retail Revolution for banks*

# Supply instant satisfaction.

### What is the number one Value-maker in the Information Retail Revolution?

*Supply instant satisfaction.*

Why wait for satisfying a need? The consumers wants it now. Anytime. Anyplace. Why? Because she can. She is used to it. In all her needs. Good for her: the Information Retail Revolution made it possible.

This ability to offer instant satisfaction is by far the most important value of the new Information Retailers. Instant satisfaction makes them immeasurably better than their old online or brick & mortar competitors.

The world is starting to revolve around instant satisfaction. From my phone, I can see what time the trains are leaving, what I should eat tonight, watch that obscure clip from 1992, listen to any kind of music, know what song is playing in H&M and buy it directly, buy a car; table; boat; house; and an Indonesian stamp collection from 1948, navigate my car through Germany, order a Tikka Masala, see what concert to go to tonight, read the newspaper, see what people are saying about the restaurant I'm standing in front of, and call my son about this book.

That's on my phone now. It doesn't tell me to wait three weeks.

### How do banks perform on giving instant satisfaction?

*A wide split: very good and very bad.*

When it comes to the transactional side of banking, you have done a great job. But when it comes to the non-transactional sales and advisory aspects it's bad. And getting worse every day.

Which is equally bad for Mrs. Consumer and the bank. She hates you for it. And it costs you a fortune, where you could do it much cheaper.

### Is instant satisfaction a new element in business?

*No. It's a business principle I learned long ago from a Florida car dealer.*

In the 1980's I was on a project for a Scandinavian car manufacturer. They had asked us to develop a new strategy for their US dealer networks.

As usual, we wanted to see the frontline of their business, and visited many of their dealerships. We travelled to Ft. Lauderdale, Florida to visit their largest US dealership. The guy who ran it was the proud owner of the largest US Lincoln dealership too.

We drove onto his parking lot. Some 1200 Lincoln's were parked outside, sparkling in the blazing sun. Red, white and blue flags were flapping away in the hot sub-tropical breeze.

Just inside the entrance, three men in suits and ties were lounging on a bench in the shade of a large parasol. The guy most on the left stood up and walked up to our car window.

'Hi, I'm Jim. How are you today?' he said.

"Fine", I answered, but informed him that we were here to see his boss, and -unlucky for Jim- we wouldn't buy a car from him today.

Once inside, over a mug of weak American coffee, the owner told us that we just witnessed his system.

"It's all about instant satisfaction. Every time a prospect drives unto my lot, the guy on the left stands up and attaches himself. Like Jim did. He sucks up like a clam and it is his sole task to sell this person a car. Nothing else will do. Jim knows he is not allowed to let the prospects drive off my lot in the car they came in. The only way they can drive home is in one of my new Lincoln's. If Jim fails in that task, he is fired. On the spot."

"But if the prospects aren't ready to buy a car yet, what happens to unlucky Jim?" I asked.

"The only escape route for Jim is to let his sales manager have a go at his unwilling prospects. Only if the sales manager fails too, Jim is off the hook."

Jim knew about this policy, all based on selling instant satisfaction. A win-win situation, client happy, company happy, great sales-rates, great productivity, low costs, which could be converted into low prices.

How far this policy went, we experienced a little later.

The owner took us on a proud tour around his huge dealership, together with his senior sales manager. While were chatting, Jim came in again, made a beeline to the sales manager and whispered something in his ear. The sales manager nodded and off went Jim again.

'What was that about?' I asked.

'Jim asked which rental car to give to his client...” the owner replied; “...he just sold a car, plus a nice set of extra accessories. Good for Jim. But the accessories will take some work: the proud new owners can't take delivery of their new car until tomorrow.'

'Aha. Why the rental car? They can drive home in their own car, and return tomorrow, can't they?'

'No. Completely against policy. We never, ever let a client leave our lot in their own car. Never. We make up a story that we have found a great trade-in offer on their old car, and that it would be a waste if some fool made a scratch on their old car tonight, and ruin that juicy trade-in.”

“Why make up such a story?”

“Anything can happen, once our new clients leave our lot in their old car. They might forget about the whole idea of buying a new car altogether; feel a renewed comfort in their old heap and start reminiscing to each other what great times they had in their old, yet nice and trusted clunker. What can also happen is that they might turn into the lot of one of my competitors and get a better deal. No, thank you: we never let them leave our lot in their old car. Just giving them a free rental car for a day makes great business sense. They feel they got a great service, and we are 100% sure of the deal. Instant satisfaction pays.”

This Floridan car dealer certainly knew the power of instant satisfaction. Not only that, he constructed a finely tuned set of instructions and tools to make it practical.

# Create a symmetric relationship.

**As long as we have an asymmetric relationship with our clients, we can continue our business model, can't we, Hans?**
*Those days are fading rapidly, Jon.*

Mrs. Consumer hates asymmetric relationships. She loves the new symmetry the Information Retail Revolution offers her.

Do you feel happy and comfortable in an asymmetric relationship, Jon? Do you like being made to feel like a dumbo? Do you like breaking out in a nervous sweat, because your kitchen salesman is trying to push something incomprehensible onto you? Of course not. Nobody does.

That is why we were always looking for a 'trustworthy uncle'. That magic person, who not only knew a lot about something you knew little about, but also because he was on *your* side. This uncle turned an asymmetrical relationship into a symmetric one.

That is exactly what the Information Retail Revolution does. The internet has created a paradigm shift. You don't have to feel like a dumbo anymore. It broke open old asymmetric relationships. In many sectors. Not only because internet puts all these open sources of information at your fingertips, but also because new Information Retailers reconstruct and simplify their products and services in such a way that there is no need anymore for all that information.

Total transparency is total symmetry. The opening up of all information is crucial to the IRR.

There is no monopoly on knowledge anymore, the time you have to exploit an asymmetry lasts shorter and shorter. New Information Retailers *know* there is value in sharing information, instead of keeping it secret.

# Trade in needs, not carriers.

### What is the next Value maker?

*Think Need, Jon.*

Rethink what the basic *need* is that the bank is catering for. Construct your company around it. As we have seen, the Information Retail Revolution has redefined needs in a big way.

### How does it work?

*A bit of porn for bankers, Jon?*

A porn shop was a retail format. Serving a need. What need? The need for printed paper, for discs with magnetic information?

No, the basic need the porn shop catered for is sexual pleasure. Before the Information Retail Revolution the porn shop was the place to go. A magazine, a movie. And instant satisfaction too; you could enjoy a movie right then and there in a little cabin.

Porn shops are gone now. Printed paper and discs with magnetic information turned to bits and bytes. Liberating the need from the carrier. Liberating old retail brick and mortar formats to be replaced by new formats.

The same thing happened in music, where the need for discs has been replaced by the need for music. Online p2p music is serving that need a lot better than a record store. For free too!

### What is the need of Mrs. Consumer that we bankers should cater for?

*Help! How can I organise my financial life?!*

Mrs. Consumer feels very insecure in planning and handling her financial life. She feels that she doesn't have the tools or organisation to prevent big dips and peaks in her financial life. She doesn't know what financial tool-box would be best for her particular situation. She doesn't know who to turn to for organising it. She is looking for a 'trustworthy uncle' to help her with it.

She likes the ease of her internet banking and of her bank card, but she feels that the underlying need of organising her financial life is constantly slipping through her fingers.

Yes, a bank might be the obvious place to go. But the moment this thought enters her head she hesitates. She doesn't trust them to be the impartial advisor, in spite of glossy advertising campaigns. Earlier contacts with the bank have deepened her hesitation.

The crisis hasn't made it much better. There's no loyalty left. There is no reward for building a relationship. Whoever can give them a better mortgage will scoop away your customers.

In the end she accepts that, well, life sucks, her financial life will be one of those things that will stay a nuisance all of her life.

But with the tools of the Information Retail Revolution you can do what she wants, Jon.

## I may have a different take on the ultimate need that we should cater for, Hans.

*Let's have a discussion then, Jon.*

First of all, let go of traditional thinking. Then rebuild your whole business model around the need. Now it is time, the only time, to let go of the old way of thinking and successfully turn the tide. With this new thinking, the opportunities to make money can change in your favour.

In the examples in this book I offer some practical solutions.

# Make everybody a producer.

### How else could we increase Value, Hans?

*Make everybody a producer, Jon.*

Central production is going peer to peer (p2p), as we say in the Information Retail Revolution. Individuals produce, individuals consume, making huge central production facilities obsolete. We are entering a society in which production has shifted from a few in the elite towards the mass.

That is what you could do as well, Jon. Make your bank the platform for financial services of 100's of thousands of producers. That's how Apple iBank would do it.

### Please explain p2p?

*It is what my son Tom does with music and tv-shows.*

My son Tom is 19 years old. He sings and plays the guitar in a band with 3 friends. He writes a song in the afternoon, records it in the bedroom of one of those friends that same night, publishes it on the internet 5 minutes later, tells all of his friends via Facebook and some other social media at the same time.

Before Tom goes to bed, his new song is heard by hundreds of friends, friends-of-friends, friends-of-friends-of-friends. Peers to peers to peers.

The next day he hires a video camera, shoots a 10 minute comedy show with some other friends, his brother Rik edits the show on his laptop, one day later the show is put on YouTube, publicised once again on a score of social media, and seen within 24 hours by almost 10 thousand peers to peers to peers.

That is p2p. It changes the music and entertainment world totally. As it changes all Information Retail.

## Some other examples of p2p?

*Wikipedia; pure peer to peer information.*

Or eBay: p2p selling & buying. Where do you go to look for a second hand car? Online of course. Where the choice is huge, where you can buy straight from the owner.

Or real estate, which is also hit massively by p2p. Yes, the house is very tangible, but many people buy or sell their house themselves. P2p, with the help of the internet.

## It's hard to imagine p2p in the world of retail banking, isn't it?

*Not at all. It's easy.*

eBay is busy with developing p2p lending. But look up Zopa or Funding Circle too. Internet makes peer to peer lending possible in very much the same way as we sell and buy our second hand cars.

A loan is nothing more than information. It's an exchange of digital money against a contract for future payments of interest. P2p intermediaries bring together people with the money, and those who need it. All purely information, which makes it ideal for the Information Retail Revolution.

Look at what Zopa writes on it's website: "Both lenders and borrowers get better rates, because peer-to-peer lending is more efficient than the traditional banking model. Banks have massive overheads, with thousands of employees to pay and hundreds of branches to maintain. So they have to have large margins." P2p is quicker, it's cheaper, it's no compromise.

At Zopa, borrowers pay about 125 pounds transaction fee. Lenders pay a 1% annual service fee. At least, that is the price-setting for the end of 2010. The more competition will grow, the more these prices will be under pressure too. Amazingly: there is *trust!*

The Daily Mirror said this about Funding Circle: "This is really a case of power to the people and could be one of the best things coming out of the crisis. It's a win-win for both sides." Indeed; the IRR hits.

The Information Retail Revolution and crisis boosted the need to borrow from each other. The trust in banks has nose-dived. The IT

Revolution has made it technically possible. One of these new initiatives will be the new Google of financial products.

## Just a bit more about p2p lending: how does it work?

*Like this:*

You get a credit score (A,B,C or Young). Lenders make a lending offer (this much, to those people). Borrowers snap up the offers they like the look of, and post an offer. It works like an auction, (one of the Information Retail Revolution learnings too) and you can come back the next day to see if there's a better offer.

If you lend €500, you lend it to at least 50 people to spread your risk. Borrowers do the contractual things with their lenders through the site. Borrowers repay monthly.

And if there's no repay, a traditional collection agency starts the recovery process.

## Will the regulators allow p2p lending?

*Not yet.*

We can understand the fears of the regulator to let all types of informal lending go on unhindered on the internet. This is a perfect illustration of the challenges that face regulators and law-makers in a world where business models have shorter and shorter life-cycles. How can regulators allow enough innovation, if only to challenge the existing might of dominant players? How can they do that while at the same time ensuring the financial safety of its citizens?

## But we as a bank should not engage in P2P lending or P2P saving, should we?

*Why not, Jon?*

If you were a newspaper CEO, would you be in the paper-printing business? Or in the news-business? Or in the reliable-links business?

Why wouldn't you enable reliable P2P lending and saving to your consumers? Why wouldn't you redefine the need you cater for?

## P2P won't be a threat to serious banking. We have already seen some of these initiatives die.

*Don't be so sure. Ask MGM or EMI.*

Why not take the initiative in these matters, Jon? Why sit and wait for others to fail? Why just defend and react instead of being proactive? Why not conquer that P2P market on your own terms?

Will there be a need for lending in five years time? Yes. Would Mrs. Consumer take a loan from somewhere else then a bank, if it's quicker, cheaper and easier? And -not unimportant- when it is NOT a bank she's dealing with?

Don't love your format too much. It might be a strangling love-relationship. The Information Retail Revolution has turned most of Jules Verne ideas into reality over the past years. Just start by expecting the worst, Jon.

Technology isn't an issue anymore. The only important thing is the need for such a service.

# Supply the 'trustworthy uncle'.

### How else could we increase Value, Hans?
*Supply the 'trustworthy uncle', Jon.*

Financial decisions force Mrs. Consumer into the scary, unfamiliar phase of buying scary, unfamiliar products. She feels small, dumb and scared. When confronted with scary decisions she seeks the confidence of someone or something to help her over the bumps in those scary processes. If she's got an uncle who is a bank manager, she will ask him for help. Because the uncle not only knows the secrets, he is also firmly on her side. Which takes the inequality out of the relationship.

Mrs. Consumer would love such a 'trustworthy uncle' in her financial life. Just as she phones the uncle who is a doctor when she has to go for an operation. The greater the possible impact of her decisions, the more scared she is and the more she desires the uncle. If only to tell her: "…you have made the right decision.." That is why bank advisors still have a function. They can offer 'trustworthy uncles'.

### Why would she be scared, Hans?
*She feels she is entering a very unequal relationship with her bank. It's what you economists call an asymmetric relationship.*

That is not something unique for banks. She will feel the same buying a second-hand car, a new kitchen, an operation or a holiday. She knows that her second-hand car salesman or her bank advisor has more knowledge about the products, the options and the prices. She knows she is wide open for a more or less polite rip-off. She is always torn between the excitement of buying the car or house and the scary feeling of having to go through the humiliation of being in an asymmetric process.

Furthermore she knows that when things go wrong the balance of power isn't on her side either. That's true for the tattooed second-hand car salesman. But it's even more true for the huge and mighty banks. It makes her very uneasy. She'd rather not enter such a scary, asymmetric process at all. But she has no choice, now has she?

## But Mrs. Consumer doesn't treat us as 'trustworthy uncles', does she?

*She doesn't.*

She reacts to the asymmetric nature of the relationship by paying you back in kind, Jon. She will be guarded, not tell you everything, hold back information, keep secrets. Which is how she feels she can make the balance of power lean her way. Ultimately not in her interest, or yours, Jon, but have you done everything to make the relationship less asymmetric?

Does she feel that way when she buys a kitchen at Ikea? Have these Swedes not taken the asymmetry out of the relation? Wouldn't it be nice to take the asymmetry out of the process in retail-banking too? Can we not entice Mrs. Consumer to put all her cards on the table? Because she understands that doing that is beneficial for her? Can we make the relationship much more of the 'trustworthy uncle' kind?

## That is precisely why we cannot close all branches. We cannot do without face-to-face contact.

*For the time being.*

Yes, indeed, there is a need for face-to-face contact, because that is the only way you can construct the 'trustworthy uncle' bit. And, yes, the legislator demands face-to-face contact too in a number of instances. For the time being we will have to accept, and cater for, the need of face-to-face contact in the process. But the fact that you need the 'trustworthy uncle' effect is no excuse to leave things as they are in a branch, or to accept branches altogether. And just a new design job will not do the trick. You have to fundamentally deconstruct, and then again reconstruct the processes of satisfying financial needs. That doesn't necessarily mean an old-school bank branch.

And perhaps then we can do the 'trustworthy uncle' even better. Your 'trustworthy uncle' function will not keep branches open for decades to come. Don't count on it. Face-to-face contact can offer the confidence of a 'trustworthy uncle'. But does the 'trustworthy uncle' need to be 100% flesh-and-blood? Can he have electronic support? Or can he be completely an electronic 'trustworthy uncle'? Can he be a far better 'trustworthy uncle' too?

## Just to be precise: what exactly scares a consumer?

*It depends on the comfort zone of the individual.*

What is scary for one person may be a piece of cake for someone else. Being scared often occurs when the frequency of making a specific decision is low, or the decision has a long term impact. When the amounts involved are large, matters start to get scary quickly too.

Right now, banking products are kept pretty complicated. And because we only buy a few of them of them in our lives, we never get used to the process of selecting one. Let alone for people who do it for the first time. We all know that young couples buying their first home are major seekers of 'trustworthy uncles'. So at one point we need someone to tell us that what we are doing is right. But we don't need that all of the way.

## Does the internet take the asymmetry out of the relationship?

*It does.*

Would you have been comfortable buying a holiday online ten years ago? I wasn't. Now we all have access to information as good as, or even better than the travel agent in her office with the potted plant. The asymmetry is gone.

Think into the future and realise that 'complicated' will change. Scary will change. Asymmetry will change. Fast.

## Are rich or highly educated people less easily scared, when it comes to banking?

*No. The need for a 'trustworthy-uncle' knows no barriers in income or education.*

Rich or educated people are considered to have more confidence in dealing with their financial affairs. Wrong. They may display an air of confidence, but they can be as scared as anybody. When it comes to low-frequency financial decisions which have a high perceived risk, it gets scary for rich people too.

It doesn't matter if there are fewer or more zero's on their bank statement.

## Should we rethink the way we deliver our 'trustworthy-uncle' function?

*Yes. It cries out for fundamental innovation.*

It is really bad; your advisors are just salesmen. They are way too expensive, have an atrocious productivity, with appalling consumer satisfaction figures. You can supply the 'trust-worthy' uncle effect in a completely different, cheaper and better way. In normal retail banking as well as private banking such innovation is long overdue. Maybe even more in private banking, as the gap between promises and reality is even more pronounced.

## Will the need for face-to-face contact last forever?

*No. Keep your finger on the pulse.*

In many other information-retail sectors we have already seen that former face-to-face contact has been replaced by electronic methods. To much higher satisfaction of the consumer. The 'trustworthy-uncle' was replaced by the 'trustworthy-system'. Back-of-the-envelope advice replaced by system-advice. Personal relationships replaced by more satisfying system relationships.

## Does the new generation need a real human to take the scary bit out of financial decisions?

*Less and less so.*

With the influx of the new e-savvy generations, it may well be that the face-to-face need will diminish in many financial-need processes too. At what pace? With what instruments precisely? We can predict some, but be open for the wildest ideas, at the wildest speeds.

## But we need branches, advisors, chairs and desks! People need people!

*It's changing fast, Jon.*

In an interview with Quote (the Dutch Forbes equivalent) in 1989, I said that record stores where here to stay because "you'll always want to touch CDs." How wrong I was.

As we are starting to get used to the new media, we are coping quite well solely online, when buying everyday products. Most people now dare to buy music, a book or a holiday online. Young kids especially are completely confident online, especially compared to the shyness they display in most shops with sales people around.

## Real humans will become obsolete in the whole process, from orientation to delivery?

*No, but their moments of contact are less frequent.*

The IR Revolution offers us the tools to digitalise all steps of the buying process in many sectors. And when you base these tools upon intelligent analyses, it becomes better, every step of the way. We can buy more music than a record store can keep in stock, read more reviews than a book salesman can tell you about, compare many more flights and hotels than a traveling agency can, and buy any porn movie you like, without the fear of bumping into your colleagues.

### Advice through a screen? From new media? People are the knowledge of my bank!

*They aren't. No, wait. They shouldn't be.*

People forget faces, forget names. People don't know you if they haven't seen you before. People don't see how your bank account showed a big peak when you recently switched jobs, and they don't know that it might be wise for you to start saving up college money now for your future children, because 867 out of 1,000 people successfully did so before. And they aren't at the office when you are there to set up a savings account.

### Should we always deliver the remaining face-to-face trustworthy-uncle bits in offices, in branches?

*Not necessarily.*

It can be delivered by advisors in Mrs. Consumer own home. Your advisors can be based in their own home. Or in just a plain old office in a plain old office building. Where these people are based is not the crucial element. Where the roof over their head is, is not the key to this discussion.

Just plain old retail wisdom tells us that it is cheaper to let the people come to you instead of the other way around.

### So should we fire all bank personnel?

*No. But rethink their use. Give them IRR-tools.*

Linking the right product to the right people isn't rocket science. So critically rethink people. Where do I need intelligent analysing, life planning and smart accounting? And where do I need someone to tell me that I did all right, talk me through some of the hard bits, and give me a calming *latte machiato*? Use the IRR tools for the former, people for the latter. We'll get into the difference between the two much deeper in later chapters of this book.

# Repackage towards consumer needs.

### What else can I do if we want to increase our value, Hans?
*Repackage and differentiate your products to reflect consumer needs, Jon.*

Package them and name them in a way that matches how Mrs. Consumer understands her problem, dream or fear. One identical, ordinary, product can take on different appearances. That is what happens all the time in Information Retail Revolution.

### Can you give an example of how Information Retailers repackage identical products?
*The porn sector is pretty clever in it.*

Different people, different needs, as we all know. You may prefer *brunettes, mature* ladies, or ladies with *glasses*. Whatever it is, porn portals offer the choice of hundreds of such personal and different preferences. One click will bring you to your personal *differentiated* heaven. And we all know the economic law that *differentiation* creates added value. Allowing you to charge premium prices too, as the famous US economic guru Michael Porter tells us.

The porn sector understands how to create such wide-spread choice without gigantic costs. They take one tantalising picture of one *mature, brunette lady, with glasses*. Then they repackage it. You'll see that same picture on the highly specialised *brunette* site. On the equally targeted *mature ladies* site. And also in the highly valued *ladies with glasses* site. Huge differentiation at very low cost!

As we now all understand, there is a database behind such a portal. With the help of *tags* this database repackages bits of identical information.

Porn was one of the first sectors -as usual- to pick up the use of so-called tags. Tags have become a very standard tool in the Information

Retail Revolution today. You will find no blog or book-library without it today.

## Can you have a less porny example to take it further?

*A bit less sleazy? I will tell you about the Athlete Foot Principle, Jon.*

A couple of years back, we were travelling with the family through Florida in one of those big campers. We are Dutch, certainly not used to the heat, actually not used to warmth at all. Add sand and salty water, and soon some in the family (not my wife, she forces me to write here) developed a serious athlete foot condition, and a sweat induced rash in the groin area.

We stopped our camper on a huge parking lot in front of a Walgreens drugstore. Inside this store we discovered how the US is different from Europe: it is a country of self medication. A lot of Walgreens customers will never see a doctor before they buy medicines.

Walgreens is perfectly adapted to this phenomenon. They make finding the right stuff easy. All products are neatly categorised by the regions of your body; back, groin, foot, stomach, head, etc. We did some self-medication; at the foot section, we found the so-called Walgreens Athlete Foot cream. The text on the package made abundantly clear what that was. Two lanes further we found the groin cream we were looking for: it was called Walgreens Jock Itch Cream.

Outside on the parking lot I looked more closely at the packages of the two different products. It turned out the products weren't different at all. Both were Terbinafine Hydrocloride Cream 1%. I couldn't care less. I bought these pharmaceutical products for what they *do*. Not for what they *are*.

## What do we, bankers, learn from the Athlete Foot story?

*Package and name your products for self-medication.*

Financial products are enablers. People buy your financial products for what they *do*. Not for what they *are*.

That is not how banking products are named. Bankers are product-focussed. You would sell Terbinafine... etc. You develop technically advanced products, while what it does for their clients isn't complicated at all.

I've worked a lot for car manufacturers, and here you see the same thing happening. Somewhere in the eighties I was working for Volvo. Since Volvo makes cars, most of the people that work there are *engineers*. And that's engineers as in *not people's people*, which explained why -at that time- their marketing sense was pretty limited.

One of the first questions I asked the board, was: 'Why are people buying a Volvo?' Deadly serious, one of the board at the time replied; 'That's simple, because of the DeDion rear-axle.' I had driven many Volvo's, but never heard of DeDion. How many Volvo buyers had?

### How do you see this renaming of our products?
*Follow the old cigar box saving tradition.*

In Danish farmhouses they used to have several cigar-boxes with money on the window-sill of the kitchen. Clearly labeled for different saving-goals: Karin's Marriage, Peder's College, and so on.

In Holland we used jam jars for the same purpose, and I don't know what they use in your country, but the principle is the same world-wide.

### How can we copy the cigar box tradition in the age of the Information Retail Revolution?
*Two extra fields in your IT system and you can do it all.*

Add one field to rename and focus simple financial products in the way Walgreens renamed their Terbinafine Hydrocloride Cream 1%.

LifeEvents are a start for such renaming. A *Baby* Saving Account, a *Marriage* Saving Account or a *University* Saving Account. A *Starters* Mortgage, a *Second Home* Mortgage or a *Retirement Home* Mortgage. Inside could be identical technical products, but you make them understandable from the consumers' point of view.

The second field is open for the consumer. She must be able to give her own name to the product. *Karin's* Marriage Saving Account. *Our Italian* Second Home Mortgage.

That way we can offer todays version of the age-old cigar box habit. All of a sudden banking products have made a big leap from incomprehensible distant technical products to close-by, human, very understandable products. It's good for you too. Packaged products will bring huge amounts of insights to what your customers are really doing with our products.

### Isn't such repackaging misleading consumers?

*No, Not at all. Why?*

Walgreens gave me the confidence that I was making the right choice, that I got the right self-medication for my family. Even though we knew that both contained the same cream.

Seen from the bank's perspective, it helps a lot to focus on specific target groups. You would attach quite different sales-promotion gifts to the *Baby* Saving Account than to *Marriage* Saving Account, wouldn't you?

### With such an explosion of product varieties we would have to train all our staff in those multitudes of products? That would explode our sales training costs, wouldn't it?

*No. That's not IRR thinking.*

The immediate and confident match between the product and the consumer need is guaranteed by the name. That is the whole concept of self-medication. Let the client do the work. The Walgreens staff doesn't consist of trained doctors. They are not trained to understand what Terbinafine Hydrocloride Cream 1% exactly means.

In the Information Retail Revolution, where we would use the electronic 'trustworthy uncle' for advice and matching, it would be even less of a hassle. Introducing one product more doesn't put a strain on you when you apply the Information Retail Revolution Rules.

# Towards NoCompromise: the Price-creators.

**Right, now about the Price-element of the NoCompromise bank of the Information Retail Revolution. How would we decrease prices, Hans?**

*We have some tips there for you as well, Jon.*

I have described those that have the most impact on the following pages.

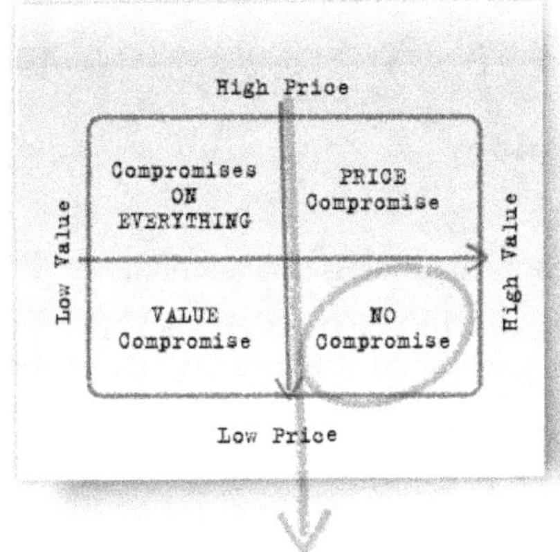


*Towards NoCompromise. The Price-element of the Information Retail Revolution for banks.*

# Pricing for needs.

**What is the easiest way to create a better price perception?**

*Price for needs, not for the basic product.*

The moment a product seems to be made for you, the consumer -made especially for your *need*- the value of the product shoots up, and therefore price-sensitivity is reduced.

But when you sell just a plain old generic product, the value does nothing for you, the transparency of the pricing increases and the price-sensitivity increases too.

**Can you explain this with an example?**

*Think Walgreens once again.*

Two packages, both with identical content. Jock Itch Cream and Athlete's Foot Cream. I couldn't remember what I paid for it back then in Florida, so I checked the prices on the internet this week. It turned out that on that day, I could get 1 oz of Walgreens Terbinafine Hydrocloride cream for $15,08, $12,06 and $9,59.

(If you want to know exactly: January 19 2011: Walgreens Jock Itch Cream/0,53 oz: $7,99. Athlete Foot Cream/0,53 oz: $6,39. Athlete Foot Cream/1 oz: $11,99.)

**Does repackaging allow differentiated discount pricing too?**

*Yes. It's what they do at Walgreens too.*

That week the Terbinafine Hydrocloride that was labeled Walgreens Athlete Foot Cream was discounted by 20%. But the -technologically identical- Walgreens Jock Itch Cream wasn't.

Repackaging allows Walgreens to price and discount each product differently. They apply the economic law that *differentiation* creates added value. Allowing them to charge premium prices. And allowing them to discount a part, but not all of the volume.

## Do we bankers do differentiated pricing like Walgreens?

*Too little.*

You behave much more like hard discounters like Aldi and Lidl did in their starting days. Offering just one variety of generic products, which leads to a very transparent pricing. There is room in the market for such hard-discount tactics for specialised banks. Look at ING Direct. But for many banks with a wider assortment that's difficult.

## We do differentiate our products with new technological inventions.

*Why not search for non-technological differentiation too?*

It reminds me of a discussion we once had with manufacturers of butter. The question was: how to raise the value of their products? Hmm, these food-engineers reacted: impossible. Butter is butter is butter. The consumer doesn't like to change the taste. And, last but not least: what does the law allow you to change in butter anyway? These engineers immediately thought of improving the *technological* quality of their product. Which didn't offer much perspective.

But as every experienced marketeer can tell you, once you think *perceived* quality, or rather *value,* things change. For a small amount of butter, say 100 grams, pressed into the form of a sheep, packaged in a nice see-through bulb, with a Christmas label, marketed at Christmas time, you can charge as much or even more than the ordinary 250 grams packets of butter.

Bankers should think more like marketeers too.

# Cut up fees and package them as Apps.

**Can we get inspiration regarding prices from Apps, Hans?**
*Most definitely. Apps offer a nice new packaging of fees.*

What to think of an App that would warn you if there is too much money on your current account and suggests you can transfer it to your saving account? If you price that at 2,99 euro, would you buy it? If many others would buy it too, you would end up with a nice sum, wouldn't you, Jon?

The new conventions that are developing around Apps is that you put together your own set of tools around a certain subject and price each individual element.

This offers a breakthrough in the eternal fee discussion for banks. You can pimp up your standard current account with an iWave planning App at 39,99 euro. Or a yearly budget analysis at 19,99 euro. Or a design your own bank-card App at 2,99. If you got more than a certain number of these Apps, you can buy the whole suite of Apps at 79,99 euro for a complete collection of interlinked apps. Just like an Album in iTunes offers itself, once you have bought a certain amount of single tracks.

# Flexible pricing and auctioning.

### How else could we decrease prices, Hans?

*Systemised flexible pricing and auctioning.*

Many successful Information Retailers use it. Travel agents, airlines, hotels, but also eBay and iTunes. They don't let their front-line people do the bartering, it is the system that does it.

Auctioning is a great IRR pricing instrument. It creates immense price-trust, and that is what it is all about. With the Information Retail Revolution, some ancient old pricing mechanisms make their return.

It's institutionalised bartering. What was possible in the one-man market stall of the past, is now possible again on a huge scale. The ordinary man becomes the producing entity in information retail. And how is the ordinary man used to doing business? By bartering. 'One size fits all' doesn't exist anymore, and that is also true for prices.

### Does it work for our small and medium size business clients too?

*Yes. Think of Workspace, for instance.*

If you have a job that needs a specialist, like replacing an air conditioner, you used to flip through the Yellow Pages, ring one that looks appealing by the ad and that was that.

Nowadays, you put the job offer on Workspace and within hours you get the first bids by contractors. And because they outbid each other, you get a good deal. That can be equally true for retail banking.

### In banking? Bargaining?

*Many financial players already use it.*

The Information Retail Revolution has opened up a whole new financial democracy. Question and demand in it's purest form. Don't like the price? Come back later or try someone else. Serving individuals, as we've learned, isn't expensive anymore. People can bargain all they want.

eBay was one of the first. You can buy anything at eBay and it all happens through auctioning. But also new financial players use it. Like Funding Circle.

There are two ways this works as a lender. When you sign in you can transfer money into your Funding Circle account and set up 'Autobid'. Autobid bids on loan requests from businesses and existing loans from other lenders. You use the slide bar to set the return you want and click OK. You can also tell them the Lending Speed, adjusting rates to get quicker results. At any point you can adjust these settings.

The other option is to bid on individual loan requests. You can view and filter all loan requests that have gone through the credit rating process. Say you've found a nice food and drinks shop in London that needs a loan. Click it, and you'll see the list of offers by other lenders. You can instantly make a bid, by entering an amount and interest rate. Once there are sufficient bids to fully fund the loan, new lenders may bid a lower rate, knocking out other lenders bids.

And, just like with a real bank, you can sell your loan in parts to others.

# If it can be free, it will.

### How else could we decrease prices, Hans?
*By being free.*

If it can be free, it will. When so many people can produce and distribute, there will always be some clever fool who finds a way to drive down the price. Even do it for free. In the Information Retail Revolution many things are free. Even very valuable services.

We all use Google. But do we pay anything for it? We don't. There are many like Google, who offer their services for free.

### We offer our advice for free, don't we?
*That's right, but is it of the same high quality and independence as Google maps?*

If you were to bring your advice to that same level of impartial, trusted high quality as Google maps you would make a welcome post-crisis change to a market crying out for that kind of advice.

### Can we learn from other Information Retailers about this?
*Let's look at porn again. The Information Retail Revolution has toppled their earning model.*

In the old days the Hollywood-based porn kings produced 10 thousands of movies per year. Today there are millions of porn movies on the internet. That drives down the price, as any economic law will tell us. Then there is piracy of official titles. Conclusion: nobody pays for porn anymore.

That forces the porn industry to find new ways to earn money. One way they try is to pay each other for links. But it is difficult. One business model is following the other in an ever-increasing jumbling of ever-shortening life-cycles. Each of which reduces the earning potential.

In the summer of 2010 we even witnessed strikes by Hollywood porn stars against their declining incomes.

### How can we ever earn money in this revolution?

*That's a valid question, Jon.*

For years now, companies are struggling to find the right business models to this revolution. The answer to this seems as simple as it is difficult. If a retail format can be free, it will.

### So, what can we do with this lesson?

*Don't believe in anything other than serving the pure need.*

Soon banking will be a pure technological affair. Linking people together through the web and offering lending and saving services has proved to be easy. So charging for these services because you have to pay your employees and rent won't be tolerated much longer.

# The PPMMC rule.

## How do we orchestrate all Media, all channels in the Information Retail Revolution-times?

*Make music with the new version of the good old PMC: the PPMMC.*

We all know the Product-Market-Combination, don't we? That good old PMC is not precise enough anymore to describe today's multi-channel reality. That is why we have added a P (for Phase) and an M (for Medium). With that PPMMC we can make music.

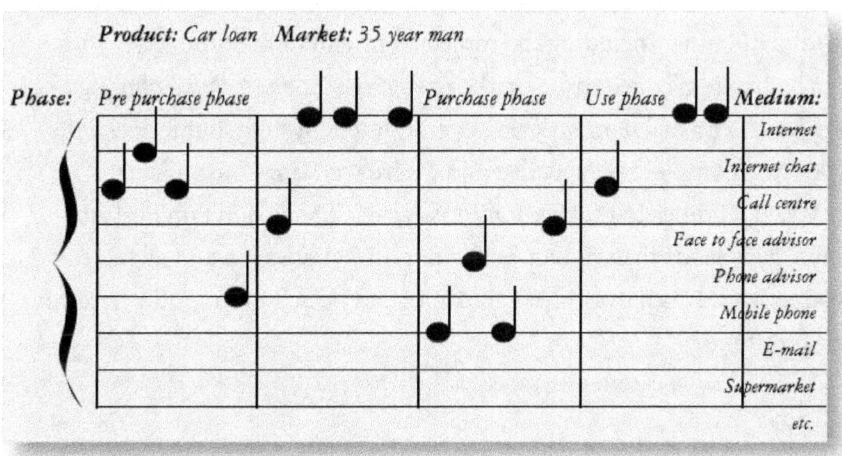


*The PPMMC rule of the Information Retail Revolution-age. Just an example*

That PPMMC has proven to be a great tool to deconstruct and then again reconstruct the process your customers go through. From the beginning to the end of the LifeTime of the Product. As seen from the perspective of Mrs. Consumer.

## How do you define the letters that make up the PPMMC?

*Product*

Not much different from what it was in the PMC, but defined in the most fundamental way: the Need of the consumer. Sexual pleasure. Not a DVD. Music. Not a CD. A home. Not a mortgage. Think Life Events.

*Phase*

That is new. Cut up the complete process of a product into individual phases. As seen by Mrs. Consumer. The *pre-purchase, purchase* and *use* phase. It starts with her first inkling of an impulse, goes through getting advice, up to the purchase itself, then through to the use of the product in its total life time. Including the replacing or end of the product.

You bankers concentrate on the *use phase*. The *purchase phase* gets less focus. You call it an ordering or fulfillment system, but it doesn't reflect the complete perspective and desires of Mrs. Consumer.

When it comes to the *pre-purchase phase* banks don't orchestrate much. This leads to caveman-behaviour, dissatisfaction and awful productivity. It is in this phase that a lot can be achieved. And where you can profit most.

*Market*

Describe target audience, just as in the good old PMC. Are we talking about a market of poor pensioners, or a market of filthy rich young stockbrokers? Market has impact on the Product, that is quite clear. But it has an equally great impact on which Medium each Market chooses in each Phase. Orchestrating that mix into a PPMMC that's right for a specific market is crucial in the Information Retail Revolution.

*Medium*

Medium describes the preferred Medium for the chosen market. We are all used to switching between a wide variety of Media. New ones pop up every year. Different markets use different sets of media.

*Combination*

All of the letters before must add up to a good combination for both Mrs. Consumer and the company. Just like the good old PMC did.

**Do we banks pay much attention to what goes on in our branches? Do we know the PPMMC's there?**

*No, you don't.*

Banks are great at 1) orchestrating the process once the product is activated and used. What goes on before that point is often undefined. Apart from some sales-training and compliance rules the 2) Pre-purchase process is vague at best.

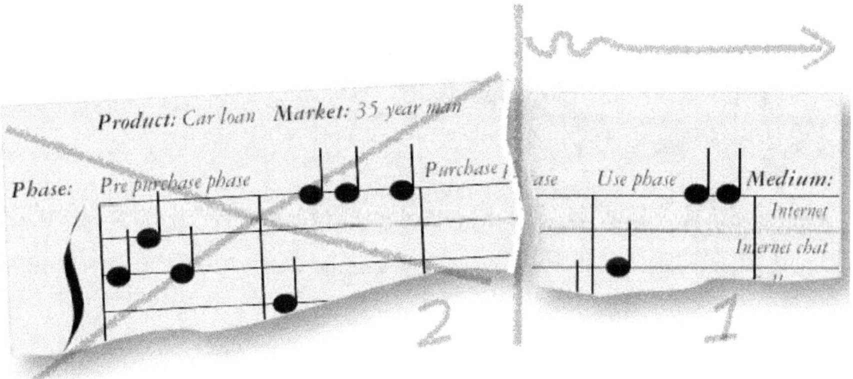


*Retail banks don't plan the Pre-Purchase, the Matching, phases well, if at all. That's what causes mis-matching, which turns out as mis-selling.*

## When you deconstruct and reconstruct, do you cut out steps too?

*Of course. That is where your main benefit lies. And that of Mrs. Consumer.*

That is where your savings will show themselves. The fact that most banks do not plan the pre-purchase phases leads to an enormous wastage of time and money.

In the processes many unnecessary steps are still present, but where wastage can be cut out is in preventing repeated sales-cycles. Think of the Marc and Vanessa story; it took them 3 tries to get the account manager on the line, and they had 2 or 3 almost identical meetings, instead of one. The point is that bankers do not analyse what goes on there. If you don't know, you can't change it.

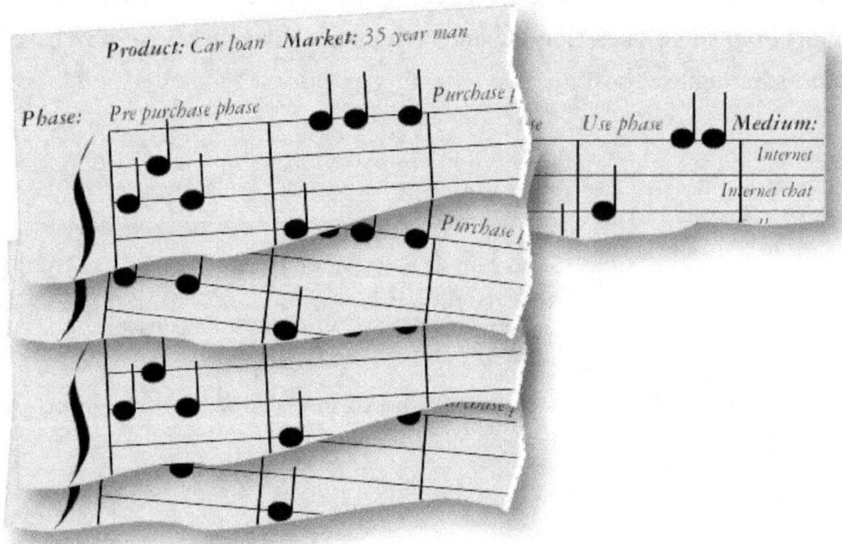



*This is what many processes in retail banking look like. Repeating sales-cycles before the product is sold. Bad for Mrs. Consumer. Bad for the bank. By creating instant satisfaction for Mrs. Consumer as the leading principle, your processes can be made much more efficient. With huge benefits for Mrs. Consumer as well as the bank.*

## What is the first thing you advise us to do, when we start on a branch-network strategy?

*Plot todays PPMMC. Analyse what's going on in your branches and other media.*

It's something we always do, when we start at a bank-client. Go out into a number of branches and spend half a day in each. Do the same for other media like the internet and call centres.

Note down what is happening. Just looking at your IT-systems will not tell you enough about what goes on at our branches. Banks are great at IT for the using phases, once the product is started. You can tell me down to the minute which clients did what on their account. But you don't register and analyse everything that went on before the start of the product. The pre-purchase and the purchase phases.

Deconstruct your own PPMMC's. Plot out today's processes. Than start to reshuffle the individual phase/medium combinations. Reconstruct the process. Be prepared to throw out many steps. It is impossible to reconstruct without applying all the tools of the Information Retail Revolution.

The next step is orchestrating the media in the PPMMC model that you then have. That requires great out-of-the-box thinking and creativity.

## Learn from a real-life Danish bank-laboratory.

# How Jyske Bank does banking.

As we have seen now, the rules & tools of the Information Retail Revolution are not just a threat. They are the key to success in retail future. By applying them yourself you can change your retail banking fundamentally. It will put the consumer first. It will enable *good*-selling. It will reduce costs. Like I've demonstrated with Apple and Ikea.

In this chapter we show you how these rules come together in the present too. In a Danish bank that has already adopted many of these learnings.

# Tomorrow's banking today: Jyske Bank.

**With iBank you sketched out the future. With Ikea too. Are there any examples of your thinking that are working already today? What can we do with our branches now?**

*Let's go to Denmark and look at Jyske bank.*

Jyske Bank is Denmark's third largest bank. A retail bank for consumers and small to mid-sized companies. We pioneered many of the lessons of the Information Retail Revolution. And many lessons from regular retail too.

**What is the size of their branches?**

*They aim to have about 20 to 30 people per branch.*

Jyske Bank pulled back from small branches already in the middle of the 90s. There are still some smaller branches around, but they focus at big branches on well-chosen locations within each region. Consumers and small to mid-sized companies are their trade, so they are at easily accessible and visible locations in the region.

# Jyske Advice.

**Has Jyske Bank put focus on the matching process? The planning phase before consumers actually buy the product?**
*Yes. This is the most crucial and costly phase.*

Jyske Bank decided, well before the Information Retail Revolution, to put all that goes on *before* the actual purchase of a product into their computers. Advice, analysis, customisation, everything. Unlike most other banks, who start the data-entry after the actual purchase has been made. Pretty smart of Jyske Bank, as the Information Retail Revolution offers them so many fantastic advice tools at their finger tips.

**Has Jyske Bank changed the way the advisor and client are talking to each other?**
*Yes. They always use what we called screen-bouncing.*

Each of the working places of the Jyske advisors has a screen, which is visible to both advisor and client. A normal screen at the consultant's table. A large touch-screen, with a connected wireless keyboard, in the meeting rooms. All Jyske client-banker interaction *bounces* via the computer *screen*. In every type of customer session. Whether it is at the team-table or in the meeting room, or in a phone conversation. No rocket science at all, just applying the way we all normally work together when a computer is concerned.

Contrary to most banks, the Jyske advisor is *not* hiding behind a computer screen, thus cannot be suspected of doing all sorts of secretive things. Advisor and client are looking at the same screen. All of a sudden the relationship is much more balanced, much more symmetrical. The client is stimulated to understand what goes on. The developers are forced to make consumer-friendly interfaces. Explanations can be done with audiovisual support. Input goes much quicker, corrections are immediate. Great for productivity. Great for instant satisfaction.

Furthermore, this is going to be the exact same system as she uses at home, so the client is within her comfort-zone and confident.

### Does the Jyske Bank system capture all data too?

*Of course. A good by-effect of the screen-bouncing.*

All interaction goes via the screen. Questions, advice, explanations, everything. Not on the back of an envelope; no transfer after the meeting into the computer. No, what goes in the system stays there. Everything that is discussed, shown, or decided, enters into the system instantly.

The interaction bounces from the advisor, via the screen to the client, and vice-versa. This **screen-bouncing** makes data-capture immediate, which does great things for accuracy and productivity. It gives the customer the safe feeling that her data are correct, are indeed in the system, and cannot be lost somewhere between the scribbles of the advisor and the moment of data-entry.

The advisor walks through the well-thought-out scenario of the meeting, using the screen as his guide. He runs through Q&A's on the screen and analyses the client's situation that way. The system shows the options. The answers go in the system and stay there. When everything is done the advisor asks "Shall we confirm it?" When he hits OK, he prints it all at once. Instant satisfaction.

The system contains all Q&A's and forms that you have to go through from the regulators and all the compliance too. In the Jyske system it's all in there, monitored and saved.

Is that revelatory in the banking world? Yes. Is it rocket science? No. Not at all: Jyske Bank uses conventions which have become very normal in the IRR.

**How do the Jyske advisors know what to during the advice-play?**

*It's all choreographed and scripted.*

Again, let the system do the thinking. The banker is there to take you through it.

**Doesn't this way of working take out all spontaneity of the advisor?**

*On the contrary.*

The advisor can concentrate on the human aspects of the discussion, because he feels secure that the structure of the meeting is taken care of by the system. He has the confidence that everything that is discussed goes into the system, so he doesn't have to take notes. At the end of the meeting his work is done, he doesn't have to do loads of administrative work anymore, which is what happens at most other banks in the world.

What do you think all of that does for his spontaneity?

# Jyske statistical advice.

### What is Jyske Advice based on?

*Statistics. Not on the uniqueness of the client.*

This is how we described the concept:

"Unlike most other banks in the world, Jyske Bank will not pretend that you are unique. On the contrary: we know you're very un-unique.

That philosophy is very much to your advantage. We help thousands and thousands of clients per year make their personal financial plans. So we constantly improve our Jyske Bank Portfolio Database. Every hour of the day, every day of the year.

Your skilled consultant uses the Jyske Bank Portfolio Database to ask you just the right questions. And to give you the right answers, quickly and surely.

That guarantees you facts, strategies, solutions and alternatives that totally match your situation. Not based on a personal hobby of just one consultant, but on experience, statistics, and sophisticated analysis-models.

And, as you have come to expect from Jyske Bank , these systems are extremely transparent and easy to understand. And so are our professional consultants.

"Welcome to our bank!"

### Conventional doctrine dictates that in bank advice the advisor should never, ever, communicate via the computer.

*Absolute and completely outdated rubbish.*

In most banks, the computer is a tool to help the employee. We turned that around at Jyske Bank. The employee is helping the system. That way he can help the client the best.

Everything is scripted. These days we are blessed with IT intelligence, which makes life as a bank employee- or customer much easier. Sadly, most banks use only a fraction of the possibilities that the Information

Retail Revolution offers. At Jyske Bank, the system contains all the collected intelligence and experience and it shares it. Like we are used to in real 21st century life

In this day and age it would be a bit silly just to rely on the wisdom of the employee. It makes processes slow and costly. Now we could easily introduce a new banking product within a day. We'd just put it in the system. In old-fashioned banks that speedy action would be followed by a long period of training the advisors. To enable them to recognise when this product would best. Which people it should fit. How to explain the new product. A huge and costly task indeed.

In Jyske Bank thinking, employees don't need that level of extensive training, they can rely on the system.

## Weren't the employees at Jyske Bank irritated that the system does so much advising?

*No. On the contrary. It makes them confident.*

Bear in mind that the Jyske Advisors live in the 21st century too. They *know* that computers can do things we mortals are incapable of doing. Jyske Advisors will rather rely on their car navigation than their wife for finding the best route to their holiday destination. Does she know the route? Can she point out the best exit?Is she updated with the latest traffic information? No, the navigation system does it much better, taking stress and irritation out of the holiday trip.

It is exactly like that at work. The Jyske system liberates the advisors for real interaction with the client. The employees are -yes- redefined. They work supported by their clearly visible team-colleagues, and by a statistical and smart IT system. That gives them other, much more valuable tasks. They can now spend most of their time looking for Life Events.

# Jyske LifeEvents.

### LifeEvents? That is not a really new concept in retail banking is it?

*No it isn't. But how many banks have really done something with it?*

LifeEvents are all those crucial events in your life that influence your financial future. Birth, education, work, inheritance, a new house. LifeEvents have been a buzz word in retail banking for quite some time now. But in most banks it stayed just that: a buzz word. No follow-up whatsoever. No tools to capture the LifeEvent. No tools to do the follow up. Jyske Bank really does something with it.

Any bank should have as its primary task one thing and one thing only: level out the financial ups and downs, the financial waves of the customers. Not many banks really do that, but Jyske Bank does.

Big wave of costs coming up in the shape of a new car? We level it out with a car loan. Big wave of income coming up because you're changing jobs with a really big salary to go with it? We know what to do with that in order to plan the future rise and fall of your financial waves.

In order to plan somebody's LifeWaves correctly we need to know a lot about our customers.

### Does Jyske Bank do the same for small and medium sized companies?

*Exactly the same.*

LifeEvents in the business of one of Jyske Banks clients are treated exactly the same way. The Jyske Employees are trained to recognise and capture LifeEvents. And given the tools to do it with.

# Jyske Teams.

### How do they organise the employees?

*In teams. And -unlike most banks- show those teams to the clients at big round tables in an open-office branch.*

This is how we described the principle back then:

"The real difference at Jyske Bank is that we work in teams. That is really different from other banks. At most banks you are promised a personal account manager. Who is never there when you try to reach him.

With Jyske Bank you are serviced by your own advisor in your own team. Your team consists of a careful mix of relevant disciplines. All team-members know you, you know all of them. All have secured and confidential access to your files. At least one member of your team is available anytime between 08.00 and 19.00 on weekdays, and between 10.00 and 15.00 on Saturdays.

The rotation of teams is slow, which promises you knowledgeable staff, at any phase in your financial life.

Welcome to our bank!"

### How does Jyske Bank realise slow rotation of advisors?

*By making their careers in the frontline.*

If you come across a talented bank employee at your average bank, and you are pleased with the way you are treated, you know for sure that your favourite employee will be moving up the career ladder soon. Moving up, means moving out. Up to the management offices, away from the front-line.

At Jyske Bank, it's different. An employee can make a career in the front line. The more experience the employees get, the more stripes on their shoulder they get. But they don't leave the front line. Sure, they may be all over the country, as a corporate banker specialised in pig farms is, or a mortgager specialised in fishermen, but they don't leave the front line.

### Is the idea of recognisable teams good for the future retail bank?

*Very much so; higher employee satisfaction, higher productivity, lower costs.*

We found out that these teams became even more self-governing than we had hoped for. The office manager had to spend less and less time sorting out employee problems. At Jyske Bank, they immediately started managing everything themselves. Holidays, sickness etc. You only need an office manager when conflicts arise. The office manager thus has become a working foreman now. He sits at one of the tables as an integrated member of a specific team.

### So if everything is pre-cooked and online, what do the Jyske Advisors do when there are no customers around?

*Be like call centre advisors.*

The preparation and conclusion work that flows out of the advice work in most banks, is reduced a lot in Jyske Bank, due to the instant satisfaction approach. Most has been taken care of in the sessions itself.

That leaves the advisors free for phone and mail contact. As if they would have been plugged into the national call centre. It's a trick we learned at Ving Travel, one of the main Scandinavian travel agencies.

# Jyske Meeting rooms.

### An open office? What if I have a more delicate question?
*Jyske bank has a wide range of gorgeous, customised and very different meeting rooms.*

A meeting room at a Jyske Bank is not just a confined and private space. It is the stage for a well-defined play. A meeting room is about creating trust, creating a relationship. Where the advisor can deploy his trustworthy-uncle play in optimal form.

Why not make these stages customised, to fit different kinds of people? In different kinds of plays? Why not make different people feel at home in differently *styled* meeting rooms? That is what Jyske Bank did. Made every single meeting room different. In a Jyske Bank branch you can find the Jyske French Café, the Jyske Board Room, the Jyske Stock Exchange Room, or the Jyske Sports Room. It's up the the advisor to match the right room to the right client at the right moment. But these are not just design-gimmicks. The rooms are filled with props to enable the play. Like the interactive screens.

# Jyske Packaged products.

**Bank assortments are pretty confusing to most customers. How have you dealt with that issue at Jyske Bank?**

*Packaged the products. Literally.*

It is a solution that we did way back in the early 1990s for Abn Amro, Postbank Holland, Postbank Norway, Citibank USA and Argentaria Spain. And we have created these concepts since for others too.

**Why did you package financial products?**

*For a number of reasons. As we described in the Walgreens example.*

Initially we thought that packaged products would facilitate the consumer's choice. It turned out it had many more beneficial effects. Just to list a few of them:

*- Everything for instant satisfaction in one pack.*

We packaged everything that was necessary for the instant sales of the product into one pack. We made the process *undifficult*. Forms of course, but also give-aways that came with many of these products. That made a huge difference in those pre-internet days, where forms necessary for the fulfillment of these products would be lying all over the branch. Forcing the product developers to re-engineer their processes in such a way that it all could fit into a pack was a major challenge, but it paid off in a big way when the streamlining cut out many unnecessary steps.

*- Tangible assortment enables consumer understanding.*

If you package your products and put them on shelves, assortments become tangible, *undifficult*. All of a sudden the consumer can shop for financial products in the way that they can in any normal store.

We cut the assortment into categories that made sense to the consumer. This did great things for the bank's development staff too. The process of *developing* and designing these packaged products, proved to be a very effective tool for rationalising assortments, clarifying products and making it all consumer-oriented.

The first time we put the existing assortment on the wall, everybody laughed out loud because of its absolute incomprehensible chaos. Products were unrecognisable, the assortment a jungle of categories and products. Packaging turned out to be the most simple management tool for rationalising assortments.

*- Giving products names that consumers could recognise.*

Banking products by themselves are not of interest. They are enablers. Packaging products forces the developers to think of names that show to the consumers what the enabler can do for them. That way you can target and focus a product to a specific target group. Load it up with specific marketing, create added value.

All it required was one extra field in the IT, which can give one product a variety of names. Giving names and thinking of the visuals on the packs proved to be a very effective management tool.

## Packaging these products, doesn't it make matters over-complex?

*No. The technical products inside are from just a small selection of modular products.*

But we made them visible and personal. Matched them to Life Events. Linked them into the electronic system. The boxes that are standing around in the branches have a bar code on them. The customers can scan this bar code and start reading and working on the product immediately at one of the computer screens in the branch. Remind you: that was not invented in 2010, but years ago.

### Is packaging of financial products still topical in todays Information Retail Revolution age?

*Very much so.*

It works wonders on all media. In a branch, but on the internet too. Look at what Amazon.com does: the titles and visuals of books give you an immediate understanding about wether the book would be right for you.

It is a trick that you can observe in telecom too, where virtual packaging is visualised in pictures of real packs.

### Does Jyske Bank still have packaged products?

*Yes. They do.*

When you walk into one of their branches you will see *real* products in *real* boxes, like a regular retail store. These packaged products feel unthreatening and *undifficult*. They talk about the dream that the product will *enable*. Not about the product itself. The Jyske Houseplan, a packet which looks like a brick, is just one good example.

On the backside of each product you will find a barcode. Scan it and instantly the screen will jump to your product. Explanatory video's are available showing the process. All consumer-friendly and taking work away from the advisors.

# Jyske Banking works.

### Does this Jyske Retail format work?

*Yes. It does.*

I asked the CEO of Jyske Bank last year how he would measure the success of their retail format. Without hesitation he replied:

"By measuring employee commitment. Profits and turnover and market share definitely went up, but you can trace all that back to committed employees. We track that, and 74% of the Jyske employees are committed, against 17% at the main bank in our country."

Everything else follows out of that level of employee commitment.

### Does Jyske bank do nothing wrong? Are they perfect?

*They make their share of mistakes, like all companies.*

But there is no denying that this bank has pioneered an integrated retail format that is very advanced and which offers many valuable lessons to others.

### If all what Jyske Bank does is so wonderful, why haven't more banks copied their learnings?

*They lack the retail-focussed culture.*

All those banks that talk about *consumer-centric* attitudes today, don't have the corporate talent for retail banking. They don't know how to make all those little details on the shop floor work. They talk about client-focus, codes and morals, but don't change their company fundamentally.

But let's not look back why others didn't do it in the past, Jon. Let's talk about what you can learn from them today.

# Jyske Bank has a mono-personality culture.

### Why has Jyske Bank succeeded where most others have failed?

*They have one and only one corporate culture: they're retail-oriented.*

Unlike many universal banks, where a lot of corporate cultures (corporate, investment, retail) fight for dominance, Jyske Bank has a long term commitment to retail banking; consumers and small and medium-sized businesses. It defines their mono-personality corporate culture.

Anders Dam, the same CEO with whom we started this process in 1996, is the CEO today. That is unheard of in the banking sector. How many CEO's occupy the driving seat for 3 to 5 years, before retiring? This Jyske Bank CEO has a discernible passion and talent for retail banking. His drive and commitment can be felt right through the bank.

It certainly helped that Jyske Bank is not a huge world-wide moloch; it is the third bank in a small country of 4,5 million inhabitants. And they have taken care to spread the shares to all their clients, creating a cooperative feeling, without being a cooperative.

### Can large banks copy Jyske Banks' success?

*Yes. They can learn and be inspired by many points.*

There are many ideas that have been tried and tested in the real market of Denmark, which will fit other banks in other countries, with other sizes too. Jyske Bank has had this working laboratory running for more than a decade, in which many risky ideas were tested in reality. Now they are not risky ideas anymore, but proven and tested.

## Learn from hard-core retailers.
# Supermarkets and banking.

Yes, supermarkets are getting more active in financial services in lots of countries. Bankers can learn from their integrated consumer-focus. By applying their huge consumer-trust and high contact-frequency they may become an impressive competition to banks, Jon.

But -good news for you- we also see a lot of supermarket banking initiatives that fail to get off the ground. Or crash soon after take-off. Or exit after a few years. Why? Most get too far outside their comfort zone. Which disturbs their normal consumer-intuition and decisiveness.

All in all: some lessons from supermarkets for bankers, Jon.

# Supermarket banking.

### Retailers that go into banking, a big threat?

*Yes and no. The timing is excellent. But many fail at doing it.*

The Information Retail Revolution is ideal for many of these supermarket chains. They can apply the Information Retail Revolution tools and link them with the huge NoCompromise consumer-trust many of them enjoy. They can exploit their higher brand trust with their large numbers of customers, and transfer it to financial services. The supermarket does not need to have the central function bank branches have in selling financial services, but could be used as just one of several media in their PPMMC. Which keeps their costs down.

But, as I will describe in this chapter, many of the supermarkets fail to make a go of it.

### Would it be a good idea for us bankers to study what makes a supermarket tick?

*Most definitely. They are the masters of consumer-centric management.*

Some 30 years ago, retailing was regarded as a low-intelligence type of economic activity. If you were a pretty good student at university, and you decided to start your career at a retail company, your fellow-students would whisper among themselves: "What has gone wrong with *him*?" Those days are gone in many countries. Retailers have become the powerhouses of economic life, sophisticated machines that have forced the former power-houses, the brand manufacturers, to their knees. Retailers attract smart people, they have a lot to teach bankers.

That's why it is a good thing to study retailers, whether they go into banking or not, Jon.

**Is consumer-intuition real for these supermarket execs? Don't they lose it when they are in the top-chair? That is what we have seen in banking.**

*It is real. I'll tell you the story of Terry Leahy, the CEO of Tesco.*

I was working in Shanghai recently, and went to one of the new hypermarkets of Tesco, the British supermarket multinational, in one of the outskirts of this sprawling city. When I got there, I bumped into the guy who was running the Eastern part of China for Tesco at the time.

"Morning Pete! Why are you here?" I asked him.

"Terry Leahy is coming in half an hour." he explained.

Who Terry Leahy was didn't need any further explanation. To all people in the supermarket business world-wide his name is enough. He is the CEO of Tesco.

"Well, I'll get out of your hair then," I offered, "...you must have loads to do."

But Pete was relaxed and took me on a tour of his new shop. He asked me to stick around, so we could have a chat once Mr. Leahy was gone.

I did, and I saw Mr. Leahy spend 2,5 hours in that one store. Observing a detail, commenting on it, improving what could be better. Walking to the next aisle, and asking a question why the grill-counter was where it was. Getting answers, and prodding for the real arguments. He was jumping back and forth between the detail of this Shanghai store and the strategy of his multinational.

It is no secret that Mr. Leahy has a talented instinct for retail, and a fine-tuned intuition. He understands consumers very, very well. That is why Tesco has experienced such phenomenal world-wide success, while others did far less well. Mr. Leahy runs a company where *consumer-centric* thinking isn't an alien concept, not a new phrase forced by the crisis, but a real and daily intuitive and shared understanding.

**What's your list of success-rules that we banks can learn from real supermarkets?**

*Here they are:*

### 1. Passion for Consumer.

Thinking like a consumer is crucial to any retailer. At every level, from the lady at the cash-desk, right up to the board-room. Information retailers have that passion for the consumer too, they did not invent it. It has always typified good retailers. Compare the focus on consumers in banks? Rare. Not internalized and often a fading temporary phase.

### 2. Retail is Detail.

That consumers are more irritated or pleased by small details than large strategic concepts is not a new insight. Board rooms at retailers discuss those small details and jump back and forth from detail to strategy and back again.

Banks? Many haven't the slightest ideas for what the real details of consumer interaction are anyway. They seldomly discuss them. They are too distant from the front-lines.

### 3. Packaged products.

Self-service has always demanded packaged, clearly labeled products in pre-planned sizes instead of vague, misty, technical product descriptions in *whatever you want* varieties.

Packaging products was pioneered by brand manufacturers in the early decades of the 20th century. It was given even more prominence by the (then) new format of supermarkets in the 1950s and is now standard practice.

Telecoms have packaged services since the end of the 1990s. New Information Retailers do it everywhere. In spite of all that, many banks still offer vague, incomprehensible products and technical mumbo-jumbo.

## 4. Transparent Assortment.

Packaged products are a great way to start making assortments transparent. Every retailer will cut his assortment into so-called categories, logical groups of products. Categories that make sense to the consumer. Plan his store around that logic. Make that logic visible to the consumer in the store. Detailed consumer-centric shelf-planning is one of the backbones of any modern retailer. That way any consumer can find his way around even the largest hypermarkets, which can offer up to 300 thousand individual items to choose from. Which is a lot more complicated than the usual assortment of a bank.

Can we say the same of banks?

## 5. From Selling To Enabling Buying.

Self-service without the interference of a salesman is nothing new at all. But retailers forget about *selling* in their store: their key interest is to facilitate and stimulate *buying*. Which is not just semantics, but a crucial difference in perspective. Mrs. Consumer does the buying herself. The retailer offers her merchandise in such a way that she can go through all the phases of the PPMMC herself. That does great things for her confidence, she feels in power, she feels the relationship is balanced, symmetric. *Selling* is a rather outdated concept in retail, and changing your thinking brings great productivity benefits too. Ikea has demonstrated that complex products can be sold without pushy salesmen as we have already seen elsewhere in this book.

But Banks? Still in the Selling-mode. Now is the time to concentrate on Enabling Buying, Jon.

## 6. Promises You Can Keep.

Nothing new for Retailers, whether they retail on the High Street or on internet. Just think of the efforts every regular retail chain puts into measuring out-of-stock. Or, on internet, to show you what's in stock, and what's not. You wouldn't like to go into your supermarket and find they have run out of milk.

Banks are great at making promises which they know they cannot keep. Or -at best- making promises, which they have never *checked* if they could keep. Think of the promise of your own personal banker, always personally available for you, which is mathematically impossible.

### 7. Think Rotation per week per store.

How many times you sell a) one specific product b) per week c) per store is crucial in all types of retail. The lower the rotation, the more costs lean on that individual product. Inventory costs of course. But also all other costs of logistics, category management, IT and training.

For banks that is no different, yet most banks don't readily know their rotation figures. But if you know that most bank branches sell just 1 or 2 mortgages per week, it starts to get clearer. Rotation matters to banks as well.

Banks often don't even register rotation figures. They know sales-figures. But not what goes on in their branches. Their systems do not register anything before the actual sale. Or the data gets lost somewhere between the branch and the board room.

Measuring the number of prospects per day would do away with many old-school concepts, such as, for instance, requiring a meeter & greeter at the door, who can "...lead warm prospects to the right advisor, who can then make the sale..." Have you ever calculated how many warm prospects walk in the door per week per branch? A handful at most. Most products are sold 1 time per week, or even less.

### 8. Instant Satisfaction.

Nothing new or revolutionary in itself. The basis of retail since ages. It's what made Ikea such a resounding success in a world where most furniture retailers still take months to deliver your furniture. What's really different today is that 'Instant' is so much more 'Instant' than it was in the days before the Information Retail Revolution.

Banks? They have no idea of the concept of Instant Satisfaction. You want that house now! When can you step in for the first mortgage-meeting? Weeks?

## 9. System Match.

Matching your products to the right customer through a system, and not a person is not a new concept either. A hypermarket with its 300 thousand choices allows you to match the mixed and diverse needs of your family through a well-thought-out system. Think of it Jon, when you go into the hypermarket, you have to juggle the virtual shopping list for tonight, for the coming weekend, for next Monday when Granddad comes for dinner, and the needs for the holiday in two weeks. Retailers put a lot of effort into helping you match what they've got on the shelves to your real or created needs.

The kitchen story of Ikea shows that in fact, a system match has become the expected thing. Is seen as of higher value than a person match. People rely more on a system than a person in a large organisation. They feel more in command, more equal, more symmetric. On top of that, the Information Retail Revolution has offered many new tools for making such a system match more accurately and at much lower cost.

Banks? They don't invest a lot in the matching process at all. It is the overriding theme of this book.

## 10. System Relation.

Regular retailer chains cannot offer you a human-to-human relationship. It's just not feasible. Even if you would like to do it, it would be impossible with the long opening hours and the part-time employees. That is a headache that you retail bankers share with your retail-colleagues, Jon. As you know, personal relationships would demand huge costs. At best, retailers have a relationship through a loyalty system, like the Tesco ClubCard, or the Lufthansa Miles & More loyalty card system. The consumer likes that.

The Information Retail Revolution offers more and far better tools for these loyalty systems today, which also go to the core of the service. It is about creating and maintaining a deep-felt system relationship.

Banks? Their systems are aimed at selling individual products and keeping risk in check, not at creating a relationship. Strange, because you banks are sitting on top of more data than any other retailer.

### 11. Multi-format Location Network. Based on one engine.

Today's retailers aren't just in stores, they jump from medium to medium in a well-orchestrated way. From internet to call centre to store. And back. Think H&M, Tesco, Ikea. They base all interaction on one engine, and use the PPMMC principle to orchestrate it all. That is how they can think in client value too.

Banks are still very stuck in very different channels, which makes creating one picture of the client very difficult. In face to face contact, the 'trustworthy uncle' function, banks think in one way only: branches with desks with people. The only thing which changes is the number of these branches.

### 12. Volume, not margin.

The good retailer thinks in volume first, in units sold. Only then do they think in margin. All their dashboards start with volume, because they know, that's where the calculation of margin starts.

Banks are less interested in volume and much more margin focussed.

### 13. Life-time client value.

Not all, but definitely the best retailers have on their dashboard a prominent display of *client value*. In all channels. Yes, Jon, supermarkets do this. Their loyalty cards offer them these data, across all channels. That's how Tesco can tell that their internet-customers are great Tesco clients in all channels. More old-fashioned retailers calculate per client per transaction per channel. Which tells many supermarket companies, that their internet-sales don't earn money.

Banks have even better data than regular retailers, but in spite of talking a lot about *client value*, most banks that I know of, are incapable of registering total client value over a life-time. Let alone acting on it.

## 14. Mono-personality corporate cultures.

Retail groups who are in all types of retail, with a wide range of very different client groups, are hopelessly outdated and not capable of being competitive to *lean and mean* one-business focussed retailers. It gets even worse with those ailing retailers whose organisation chart resembles a spaghetti of many retail-formats, wholesale companies, and factories.

The focussed retailers have one earning model and one only. That focusses all departments, whether it is in buying, logistics or store-planning. That way they can create the highest value at the lowest costs.

Yet many banks believe they can run such an incomprehensible spaghetti-like company. Who are we kidding, Jon?

# Think franchise.

**When you talk regular retail, you also talk franchising. Do you believe we should own all of our branches in the future?**
*No.*

Working in retail for many years has taught us there are only two ways to properly run a business in service retail. Either fully independent or as a very tight franchise.

Most banks are organised as a closed chain. The branches are under one ownership and one management. The banks' employees are on the payroll of that bank, their highest boss is the CEO of the bank. The bank owns all the brick and mortar.

That model doesn't fit the trend for organising service-retail.

**What would be the ownership structure of the branches of the future?**
*A tight franchise. It's the logical solution in service retail.*

We have concluded earlier in this book that we need brick & mortar outlets not for its brick & mortar, not for tangible products, but as places of facilitating the human factor into the PPMMC's.

That means inevitably that we should search for the best ownership structure to make that happen in the best way and at lowest cost. In all other service retail sectors where human interaction is a large part of the service-offer, franchise is the ownership structure of choice.

With today's tight IT systems you see that very tight franchise systems are spreading in all kinds of retail. In product retail you see it working on both ends of the scale. Either a closed chain or tight franchise on one end, or fully independent on the other.

## So why are we retail bankers reluctant to adopt franchising? Why do we tend to keep on clinging onto our own branches?

*They made perfect sense in the past.*

In the days of the past when risk was assessed locally, when tangible money was handled locally, you could not take the risk of a franchise. Those days are fading away rapidly. Modern franchise formats define all core-functions down to the last detail. It makes sense to look at the possibility of franchising with fresh eyes.

If you organise your franchise-format well, you may get much more productivity out of them, at substantially lower costs. And with the instruments of the Information Retail Revolution you can achieve that with great accuracy and control.

## It is not completely new thinking. Many banks around the world have independents selling their products?

*I know. But you can hardly call that a tight franchise.*

The way these independent deals work is that they are based on production. 20% discount if you sell over a thousand. Exclusive supply contracts or bonuses when you make a nice turnover. It would be like the McDonalds branch around the corner only had a deal with McDonalds Worldwide that when they sold a thousand burgers, they got 200 extra for free. And that is not what McDonald's is about at all. They are extremely clear what they want in all details of the client experience.

## You see the future of banks more in the way that McDonalds runs its franchise organisation?

*Very much so.*

McDonalds doesn't own a single burger factory. Not one. Did you know that? They don't own a truck, don't do any delivery and logistics themselves. They don't have warehouses. They don't own the branches. What McDonalds does is concentrate on the choreography of the customer experience. Their earning model is based on that as well.

The outlets are owned by the franchise-takers. The factories of the burgers, the bakers of the buns invoice directly to the franchise-takers. So do the suppliers of kitchen inventory. McDonalds charges a management fee to the franchise-takers.

## The choreography of the customer experience?

*The guys at McDonald's pre-think what a customer should experience. Plus the tools to create that experience.*

McDonalds makes the menu, introduces new products, defines the recipes, and says how many seconds the burger must stay on the grill. McDonalds decides what the people wear, what they say and when and even how often they smile. All of that is their core business. They don't bother with building factories. The burgers come from local food manufacturers. Within -yes- tightly defined recipes.

# Supermarkets outside their comfort zone.

**Back to supermarkets, Hans. Not all retailers that go into consumer banking turn it into a success, do they?**

*No, they don't. Most are way outside their comfort zone.*

Supermarkets or department stores aren't God's gift to mankind when it comes to financial services. And that is an understatement. In fact, most of them screw up selling comprehensive banking services majestically.

**What are the most common mistakes that retailers make when they do banking?**

*- Wrong level and/or function in the company.*

In many supermarket chains you will see that financial services are delegated two or three levels down from the executive board. That way the project never gathers enough clout to push the culture-changes through, on which successful financial retail is conditional.

Some companies do put it at executive board level, but give it to the financial director. Why? Because he is the money guy. He deals with banks… So he knows how to retail financial services? Ludicrous. If he is a good financial director, he is completely unsuited for retailing and marketing financials.

*- Just playing around with it.*

Financials in supermarkets go in and out of fashion. That is reflected in the lack-lustre way projects are run. Not as line-functions, but in vague project-teams, fizzling out after some years of unfocussed bumping around.

*- Not connected to the core-business.*

Tesco has their financial product leaflets at a prime location in the store: more than a metre of valuable shelf space at *every* cash-desk in the country. All categories in the company would kill for that position. But Tesco has made the people in their grocery business understand the value

of financial services: Customers with financial services have a
substantially higher *total* value. They buy more of your grocery-categories.
*- Not connected to the loyalty system.*

Start with your loyalty card. Add on payments to it. Step up with
simple product-credit via the card. Then step up once again to heavier
financial products. That is the way to go. You increase overall value and
the loyalty system is a great entry-tool. Many supermarkets keep loyalty
and financials separate and pay for that terrible mistake later.
*- Selling out to a service provider.*

There are many service providers around where a supermarket can
outsource their financial services. Many are just amateurs, only a few are
really up to it, but these tend to have a completely different goal than the
retailers. They are after as much credit as possible, while retailers want to
maximise core-business turnover. Undefined joint ventures are set up by
retailers who normally are excellent buyers, without a firm grasp on why
they should have financials at all.

## So we retail bankers should not worry about retailers & financial services?

*On the contrary. Stay vigilant.*

Retailers can pick off chunks of specific financial markets with great
success. Credit cards with loyalty systems can hurt. Consumer lending on
the products that they sell in their stores is pretty common. And some will
succeed where they failed in the past. The Information Retail Revolution
offers them tools that were not possible or way too expensive in the past.
You may not define what these retailers do as banking, but it doesn't
matter what *you* call it: they are eating away at your markets.

# Inspiration from South Africa.

**Can you give some examples of successful retailer-integrated financial services?**

*Take South Africa. No retailer could survive without them.*

Retailers of furniture, home electronics, fashion, or building material would not last a week without integrated financial services. But also department stores, hypermarkets or cash & carry wholesalers offer financial services.

This is by no means limited to South Africa. Go to any DIY store in Britain, Germany or France, and you'll see in-store advertising for their credit-cards and other financial instruments.

**Surely South African retailers do not offer financial services to the unbankables?**

*They do. They are huge in money-transfers.*

Which is the number 1 financial product for the almost 50% unbankables in South Africa. Chains like Shoprite are huge in it. The supermarketeers love the money transfers, because at the end of each month it creates huge traffic to their store.

**Can South African retailers offer saving accounts to the unbankables?**

*They do. They call it 'lay-by'. It's a saving-account-light.*

A young South African sees a pair of beautiful yellow sneakers in a store. He cannot afford it now, and he doesn't want, and/or, is not eligible for a loan. He puts down some Rands, which is written up. The yellow sneakers are put in a store room for him. Next week he comes back, puts down some more Rand.

That goes on for as many weeks as he needs to reach the ticket price. Then the yellow sneakers are his.

**But this lay-by is chicken-shit, isn't it? Just small amounts?**

*Not at all. It can be tens of thousands of Rands too.*

When we were working in South Africa we saw it early one morning in Johannesburg, when we visited a store of one of the large South African DIY chains. Lots of building in South Africa is done by the so-called 'bakkie-builders', self-employed builders. A bakkie is a nice Afrikaans word for the pick-up truck, which is their most important investment.

The bakkie-builder gets money up front from his client, to build -let's say- an extension to the house. The bakkie-builder has no bank account, and certainly doesn't want the money lying around in his humble house. That's why he drives to the DIY store and puts that money into trust there. The amount is written in the book and from then on the bakkie-builder buys material from that store. Until the amount is used up.

That is really what a savings account is all about, isn't it?

# Slow erosion of retailers can happen to banks.

### Pff! We bankers build trust relationships! A supermarket chain is just in and out of the door!

*Complete rubbish, Jon. The trust consumers have in them is immeasurably higher than that they have in banks.*

A NoCompromise supermarket chain does everything to build long lasting relationships and unprecedented trust. Their loyalty cards are a major way to track what the value of each relationship is. The frequency of the contact with the customer makes that many big-name retailers enjoy a very strong and very trustful relationship with their customers.

Because they prove every week that they are the NoCompromise offer.

### Okay, non-bankers like retailers may pick off some small business from banks. Hardly a threat?

*Be careful. Department stores collapsed because of such slow but steady erosion.*

Department stores were Kings Of Retail in many countries until the 1990s. New formats like discount stores, hypermarkets, boutiques, shopping malls or specialised chains started. They never attacked the department stores frontally, but picked off more and more business year by year. At lower price-levels because of lower cost-structures. That is what drove department stores out of business in many countries.

### Do retailers follow long-lasting banking strategies?

*Not always . Think of Marks & Spencer or the US department stores.*

Marks & Spencer used to have a huge financial services department, with integrated product offerings, growing from loyalty to simple merchandise credit, right up to large mortgages. All stemming from their powerful client-card base.

Two influences made M&S sell their financial services: the guy who had built this activity left the board and M&S' core business got bad results. Time to sell off the financial business and prop up the core business.

We have seen the same in US department store chains over the years. In-out. In-out.

# Tesco may make the difference. Or not.

**All supermarkets and bankers are looking closely at what Tesco is doing. They are successful with so many new initiatives. Will they create the BigBang and change supermarket banking forever?**

*They may. Or they may not.*

To most regular retailers, financial services are outside their natural comfort zone. Retailers earn their money when the product is sold and the consumer walks out the door. That sales moment is only the *start* for bankers. They earn their money in the -hopefully- long years of use of the financial service.

Supermarket execs check their performance every month, every week, every day. Unless you translate the earning model of the financial services in such a way that it fits the normal performance-perception of the supermarketeers, it will not fly.

This clash of cultures may just be one bridge too far for Tesco too.

## Tesco might just make the difference?

*Without underestimating Tesco's talent: wait and see.*

Retailers -just as bankers- should avoid multi-personality disorders. It may be that financial services may create just that. Tesco has had an extremely talented and powerfull CEO in the past 10-15 years: Terry Leahy. It might be that his successor is less talented in managing a multi-personality company. I don't know. But don't count on it. Be vigilant, learn from how they do it.

# Keep the playing field level.
# Other sectors have regulators too.

Bankers tend to complain about the strict regulations and compliance rules. Even more so after the crisis. But rules and regulations keep the playing field level in any economic sector.

We don't dislike that as consumers. We like it that an independent authority looks after our interests in food, medicines and cars.

Why would it be any different when it comes to our financial needs?

# A regulator levels the playing field.

### Regulators and compliance are big issues for us bankers, Hans. How do other retailers regard regulators?

*Mixed feelings, Jon. But not as opposed to rules as you bankers are.*

Let's take supermarkets. Food authorities in most countries guard your health as a consumer by testing & licensing new food products before they are allowed onto the market. They also check the total process that brings the products to your table.

Of course, a supermarket CEO doesn't always like inspectors hitting his supermarkets to check if the cooling is at the required low temperature. But at the same time they like the fact that the food authority keeps the playing field level. Cooling & freezing costs are the largest cost-components of a supermarket. Which makes the temptation to turn the coolers a little less cold not unrealistic. They like it that the competitor is checked too. That's how an unscrupulous competitor can't get away with lowering his costs substantially and hitting you with lower prices. That's how you don't get tempted either.

### Should consumers be smart enough to sniff out wrong financial products? Let the market do its work?

*No. The consumers are not smart enough.*

Just like you and I are not smart or educated enough to sniff out wrong medicines when we go to the pharmacy, Jon. We consumers expect and trust that our medicines are tested by an independent and professional authority, before they are allowed onto the market, don't we?

The same applies to our cars. We don't have a doctorate degree in car engineering to determine if it is safe. We trust an *independent* authority to do that for us. No car-manufacturer can bring a new type onto the market if it is not extensively tested, licensed and therefore declared safe by them.

Why would it be different for financial products? Who has the doctorate degree in financial design to determine if it's safe? Shouldn't we trust an *independent* authority to do that same rigorous testing and licensing for our financial products?

# Self-regulation needs a real market.

### Did governments save other victims of the Information Retail Revolution?

*No. They allowed the market to clean out obsolete formats.*

Ask the bosses of EMI or MGM. Ask porn-kings, or CEO's of CD-store chains, or video-rentals like Blockbusters. They weren't that lucky. The market did its work there.

### The market didn't work for banks?

*That's an understatement. It's not a real market.*

That market was severely disrupted with obscene amounts of emergency loans. The Wall Street Journal of 3 december 2010, calculated that the US government had given 3,300 *billion* US dollars in emergency loans to banks during the crisis-period. I did some quick calculations with that number, and it took some corrections to prevent my usual mistakes with the dazzling number of zero's.

There were some 307 million inhabitants in the USA in 2010, and about 2,6 people per household. That means those emergency loans come down to almost 28 thousand dollars per household. Put the burden only on the 66% of the Americans that own their own home? More fair? Okay, than it runs up to 42 thousand per home-owning household. Wikipedia tells me that the median income in the USA is about $43 thousand per household. So there you are: we're talking 1 year of household income in emergency loans.

Quite a rescue operation, isn't it? Can the market do its cleansing job with such disruptive amounts of money?

## Shouldn't we be able to take care of our own sector? Self-regulation?

*Do you trust your supermarket, pharmaceutical or automotive colleagues 100%, Jon?*

Do you trust them to never cut corners? Will they never be tempted to look the other way when they find a possible snag in a new product? After they have thrown 100's of millions into that project already? When the figures for the next financial quarter don't look too rosy? When they are under scrutiny from aggressive analysts? When competitors show much higher share value? When their board is breathing down their neck? Do you still trust those colleagues of yours to always think of your interests anywhere, anytime?

I like it that there are checks and balances in the food, pharmaceutical and automotive systems, Jon. So do you.

## Ineffective regulators.

**Do you feel our regulators are effective enough?**
*No.*

Not rocket-science, as the crisis has proven that they were pretty ineffective in spotting and preventing the structural errors in the industry. They are regulating the past, not today, and certainly not the future. The balance of power is completely against the regulator too. Just a few smart though under-paid people at the regulators against *legions* of at least equally smart and over-paid legions of lawyers in the banks.

**But, Hans, you know that our advisors in our bank must use the official compliance form from our national regulator? We do what is asked from us.**
*Who are you kidding, Jon?*

These official compliance forms are used like policemen in american TV-shows use the Miranda warning: "...you have the right to remain silent. Anything you say can and will be used against you in a court of law..."

After which they start hitting you with the real interrogation.

# Missing the first stones.

**But haven't governments and regulators put up more demanding risk rules and don't they want to break down those great molochs of banks?**

*Nothing wrong with that. But they are missing the risk these first stones are threatened with.*

National banks are demanding that banks put more money in their coffers to act as safe-guard for new risks. Which is not a bad thing at all.

Breaking down the great molochs is not bad either. But the governments are missing the main reason why they should do so. They look at breaking up the risk. I look at breaking up cultures, Jon. As long as an explosive mix of opposing cultures can continue in banks, we will continue the risk of a second crisis.

**Well, now banks have been saved by the governments, directly or indirectly, the worst is over. Business will be back to normal pretty soon.**

*Really? Now the domino-stones are back up, they cannot topple again?*

Yes, it is lucky for the financial systems that governments picked up the toppled domino stones at great expense and have been frantically busy putting them back in their place.

While the stones were still rat-tat-tatting down, governments furiously pushed mergers and dropped in obscene amounts of cash, all to block those stones toppling further down the globally snaking lines.

They succeeded for the time being, there are still stones standing upright.

**There must be governments and regulators that are aware of the need of preventing the first stone to topple over.**

*That's rare. And even if they do, they fail to act on it.*

In discussing my analysis with governments and regulators, I invariably hear: "Yes, we are aware that not knowing the client and the risk of mis-selling is real."

But they don't give it the priority it needs. Instead I experienced a merry-go-round of "Yes, we are aware of it, but it's not our baby". That merry-go-round has taken me from a ministry to financial authority to the national central bank to parliament. And back again. Nobody is taking responsibility.

What also happens a lot is making macro-economic excuses to keep clear of actions. One thing always has to do with something else, which can keep the discussion alive for years, without real action.

But the worst excuse for not doing very much is giving in to the blackmail of the financial sector. "We cannot be pressing too hard, it will drive our financial sector out of our country..."

# Wrong banking products?

**Wasn't the crisis started because wrong banking-products were sold?**

*Wrong banking products? Or products with the wrong matches?*

How many banking products are really fundamentally wrong or dangerous? Yes, there are indeed some criminally crooked banking products about. But most banking products do a perfectly good job when matched to a well-diagnosed, well-defined, very specific, target group.

**Not a wrong banking product? What about those that loaded a huge income-insurance product onto an innocent consumer who came in the door for a simple mortgage? How would you call that?**

*Mis-Matching? A right product for the wrong person? In the wrong doses?*

Yes, indeed, there are income-insurances that are crooked. But for some people in some cases a certain dose of *uncrooked* income-insurance is just perfect. But if you mismatch them, and -driven by huge bonuses or commissions- you just heap on enormous doses of the crooked variety onto people that don't really need it, then yes, these income-insurances can cause very unhealthy and sometimes even lethal effects.

**And the totally superfluous income-insurances that were sold to the innocent Mr. & Mrs. Consumer as part of their mortgage?**

*Didn't help either.*

Yes, in quite a few instances cynical and pushy salesmen (don't call them *advisors*) unloaded these insurances on Mr. & Mrs. Consumer. These insurances were meant to counter the effect of a potential loss of their income through illness, disability, unemployment and the like.

But it was not uncommon for these insurances to carry massive commissions, or management fees. For which Mr. & Mrs. Consumer were paying. Which meant that the remaining amount of money that went to the insurance was disappointingly low.

Indeed, this often was worse than mis-selling. It bordered on legalised theft. In any case, these practices didn't contribute to the ability of Mr. & Mrs. Consumer to pay back their mortgage.

**And what about these investment insurances scandals in many countries? Why do insurance companies and banks have to pay compensation now? Doesn't that prove that they have sold wrong banking products?**

*They have done worse than that. What they have done is gross mismatching on a massive scale.*

For some people in some circumstances an investment insurance may be just the right solution. For most people it isn't. In the UK it was the wrong solution for some 5 million (!) owners of such investment insurances, who are up for compensation now. Not a typically British problem, though. It is happening in other countries as well. Large numbers of owners of such investment insurances are in now in long-running conflicts with their very respectable insurance companies or banks.

We all agree that something did go wrong on a massive scale. But what really went wrong? Was the product wrong in itself? In most cases not. It was the *matching* that went wrong. The salesman didn't check if these products were right for you.

Did he check if you realised that you were saving in shares and not in a boring saving account? Did he check that you understood that shares go up *as well as down*? Did he check if you felt comfortable with riding in that roller-coaster of the share markets? Did he check if you realised that this roller-coaster ride may pose a real risk for you?

Did he check that you understood that an investment insurance is typically a long term instrument? That, like a roller-coaster, getting out half way may turn out to be a very unpleasant and costly decision? Did he check that you realised that the yearly fees would eat up quite a bit of the returns? Last but not least: did the salesman check if you could keep up the monthly payments till the end of the ride?

In the UK and other countries you are now up for compensation if you can prove that the salesmen didn't ask one of these questions, if he didn't check if the product matched your financial health and personality.

The fact that some 5 million Britons are now up for compensation means that there was mis-matching on a *massive* scale.

## So there are harmful financial products?

*Yes. Of course. But they didn't cause the toppling of the stones that led to the crisis.*

When the *costs* of your investment insurance is so high, that its eats up almost all your returns, the chance that your invested money will actually *grow* is very slim indeed. I call that a harmful product; take it off the market by all means.

Or when you wanted to put your money away for a rainy day, your financial salesman may have talked you in one of those *structured* products where your expected returns are far *lower* than an ordinary saving account, but your risk is significantly *higher*. Well, such a product matches no-one and harms everyone too.

Please, by all means: keep them out of the marketplace.

**Politicians and regulators should look less at the wrong banking products and more at the matching process?**

*They should do both. But they consistently forget the matching.*

A member of parliament came to talk to me about the crisis. She was all fired up about 'banning wrong banking products', and wanted to push legislation to outlaw them.

"Which products are you talking about?" I asked her. I had to wake her up from her dream, and tell her that she should concentrate on the mis-matching, on the deficiencies in the diagnosis & therapy process. That she had to look at good-selling. I told her it feels nice and makes nice headlines to bash the 'wrong financial products', but it doesn't make much practical sense.

Whether she really changed her approach? I don't think so.

**Conclusion: rules and regulations aren't all bad?**

*No, they aren't.*

It keeps the playing field level. Weeds out naughty competitors. Keeps you on the honest path, delivers you from temptation. That's what supermarkets think too.

# Change is difficult.
# The next 5 years are the hardest.

The long-term vision is relatively easy to create. You can learn a lot from other retail sectors. Apply the rules of the Information Retail Revolution. Keep your eye on the most constant factor: the consumer.

The headache is in deciding how to get from A to B. To turn a ship in a storm is a dangerous idea. How to prevent the cannibalisation of existing business? The most difficult period is that of the next 5 years. How to get from today's situation into that new world?

# Vision is easy, getting there is difficult.

### What is keeping us back? The long-term vision? Or the next 5 years of change?

*The next 5 years.*

The long-term vision is relatively easy to create. The direction is pretty clear. Although we can not pinpoint quite precisely where we may be in 5 years time, the one overriding destination is always that of the consumer. In spite of technological advances she will need to level out the waves of her financial life in ten years time just as she does today. Creating the formats with which to serve her is therefore relatively easy, especially because we can learn so much from other Information Retail sectors that are ahead of banking.

Getting through the next 5 years period of change is the most difficult. But waiting is an option you don't have.

### Can we learn from other retailers what the biggest hurdles are in that period of change?

*Fear of cannibalisation. Who is the first to close the stores.*

Look at book store or home electronics store chains that are collapsing right now world-wide. They all saw the new players coming. At first they didn't regard them as a threat. When they did, the discussion about a serious change to their multichannel presence heated up. When they seemed to reach the decision to go for a serious internet presence, the fear of cannibalisation of the existing stores, popped up. No decision made. A year later the same discussion was resumed with more urgency. The discussions got more and more heated.

Then, one day, it was too late to change direction. They failed.

# The IT legacy.

**Have you thought about the IT-Spaghetti we have to work in? It's all very nice & easy that you're talking about life-time client value, jumping back and forth between media and working with a complete picture of the client. But our IT systems just don't allow that. Tying all those dozens systems together in our bank is just impossible.**

*You will have to change the legacy systems one day, won't you, Jon? It's a matter of when, not if.*

The systems you work with are getting more and more obsolete every day. There will come a time that you will have to change them. Or better: start from scratch. When? In 10 years? In 8 years? Next year? I don't know, but it's inevitable that one day you will. If you don't, which of your competitors will start to change? Who has started already? Which new player will start from scratch? Without the burden of legacy systems?

**Such IT enterprises cost a fortune.**

*Less than the fortunes you spend on your branches.*

McKinsey Belgium recently published a research among dozens of retail banks in many countries. They analysed that 49% of the costs of the average European bank is in their distribution. In their branches. On IT they spend only 11 or 12%. Well, that makes is pretty easy to me.

If you spend 20% more on IT during the next three years, which will raise your IT-costs temporarily to some 14-15%, it will allow you to decrease the distribution costs substantially. To half of what they are today? A third? A quarter? That would mean that your total costs can be taken down by at least 25%. And probably much more.

**Can such reductions be real? Can you keep up value too? Are there lessons to be learned from other information retail sectors?**

*Yes, it's very real.*

The linked-based internet, which is where you don't own the content, but the links, makes increasing value at minimum costs absolutely possible. Isn't that what the IT Revolution was all about?

Don't pin me down on the last figure, Jon, but is my logic way off track? I don't think it is. Look at the new Information Retailers; their cost-levels are incalculably lower than those of the old players.

# Change costs jobs.

**Productivity would rise dramatically if we implement all of what you suggest. But that would come at a cost: it would mean laying off bank employees. That is not politically correct today, now is it?**

*Do we let the citizens pay twice for the costs of the crisis?*

Laying off bank-staff is inevitable. Just as video rentals, porn stores, CD-chains and book stores have to lay off people. Hanging on to bank branches and advisors against all Information Retail Revolution rationale is keeping jobs alive with long-term artificial respiration.

The citizens are paying for it. Twice: 1) as over-paying customers of these banks, 2) as tax-paying citizens. Do we believe in the free-market economy? How long can you prevent the inevitable changes from happening?

# Why retail banks don't get cracking.
# The multi-personality disorder of banks.

If all the lessons of the Information Retail revolution are so simple, why don't we getcracking?

What is making our changes so difficult? Consumer-acceptance? The legislator? The regulator? Or: are we ourselves the greatest barrier for change? Is the multi-personality disorder that infects many banks making worthwhile changes difficult?

Or should we adopt this simple solution: create mono-personality corporate cultures?

# Multi-personality corporate culture.

**Well, Hans, you have made your point. The Information Retail Revolution demands and enables real innovations in the front-line of our banks. Why don't we retail bankers just do it?**

*Because of the multi-personality disorder most banks suffer from, Jon.*

Bankers are smart guys and girls. Often better educated and more intelligent than many executives I meet in other sectors. But they have to work in a distorting multi-personality corporate culture, that is not conducive to retail banking. A multi-personality culture that confuses and contaminates consumer focus and the values and perspective of even your smartest managers.

The corporate culture at most universal banks is -at best- a multi-personality. Investment banking, corporate banking, commercial banking and retail banking are each competing for their own corporate culture.

Each culture requires completely different personalities of staff & management. Each commands its own set of rules. Each requires its own management style. Each is driven by its own set of earning models. Each creates its own career attraction.

These clashing banking cultures are like a multi-personality disorder. With the same devastating effect.

**Is the multi-personality disorder the reason why retail bankers tend to have such difficulty in applying even the most basic retail lessons?**

*Yes. Most banks do not have a positive and independent retail-culture.*

Even worse; the top-brass of most banks is retail-averse. It's rare to witness an active interest and intuition for retail banking from them.

**Okay, retail banking wasn't in fashion before the crisis. Point taken. But most banks have rediscovered retail banking as the safe, steady option.**

*For how long?*

Right now retail banking is hip, because it ties in with the global post-crisis desire for low-risk, down-to-earth banking. But don't bet on that for the long term. Retail banking will go out of fashion again. As it always does. Once today's management has retired the bad memories will fade. The guys that felt the bruises of the crisis firsthand will have gone. The guys that had to clean up the mess afterwards too. Will macho corporate and investment banking be most seductive once again?

In the 20 years that we have worked in retail banking we have seen it going in and out of fashion every 4 to 5 years. Core business one year and to be discontinued the next. Recognise it?

**Not the case at our bank. Everybody in the executive board looks at what goes on in the retail department positively.**

*Looks positively? Fine, but have they demonstrated an instinct for it?*

If your bank is the exception, Jon, you're very lucky. But those cases are rare. In most banks we observe a benign interest of top-brass in retail banking. That's the most positive scenario. Too often we see top-brass of banks who regard their retail banking management with some disdain. Retail is not the sexy, macho, global, daring world of investment or corporate banking, is it?

**So this multi-personality disorder is the major barrier for innovative retail thinking?**

*It is.*

Without the focus of talent, instinct and applied intuition, you will never get speedy and focussed innovation in retail banking. Having the combination of people with retail talent and a shared intuition, sets the successful retail companies apart from the losers.

In a tough, rapidly changing marketplace this trained intuition results in good and fast decisions. A receptive retail culture will ensure that decisions are implemented accurately and with speed.

It is precisely this lack of a wide-felt passion and intuition for retail which makes many banks very slow and very conservative when they have to rethink their channel mix, their outlets and their physical contact points.

Not because they are stupid, but the lack of shared vision makes it difficult to play around with new possibilities. It is why out-of-the-box thinking or out-of-sector thinking is rare in retail banking.

### Is such a multi-personality disorder typical for banking?

*No. We have encountered multi-personality disorder in all sectors. All with the same lethal by-effects.*

We have seen it work its negative effects in the world of food too. The old conglomerates of food retail, plus food wholesale, plus food production are at the end of their life cycle. They have become too slow and too uncontrollable in the face of new, agile, rapid, mono-personality competitors.

# Different banking needs different people.

**Is it a clash of the different personalities that each different banking type requires?**

*That is part of it.*

Yes, indeed, corporate banking is largely populated by long term thinkers. Who are used to clients as more or less equal opponents. The relationship is much more symmetric: the corporate banker and the chief financial officer of the client could swap jobs easily. And they do, Jan Hommen, the former chief financial officer of Philips, the Dutch electronics giant, became the CEO of ING.

When you as a corporate banker talk about meeting a *client* this afternoon, you'll meet for lunch probably. With a guy like yourself, a professional, a mighty person in a pin-striped suit and a tie. A business man. You would not be surprised if he tries to pull a fast one on you. That makes you guarded, but not nervous; you know the game; you're equals. In fact you quite like that game. You wouldn't be opposed to pulling a fast one on him as well.

But applying that same competitive attitude and pulling a fast one on Mrs. Consumer would be devastating, wouldn't it?

The investment guys? The competitive buccaneer-type; gamblers, poker-players. Proactive and aggressive. They love to use every trick to make the relationship asymmetric. They use their elbows, are very egocentric and go for personal gain. It's what the game asks for. These guys are putting a lot on the line for one huge deal, which may or may not come through this year. But when it comes, it will mean huge rewards.

Would you let such buccaneers loose on Mrs. Consumer? Will they have lost their character, once they're at the top of the bank?

### The retail banking personalities?

*People managers.*

Not gamblers. Consumer-oriented. Organisers. People managers. Hierarchical thinkers, which makes sense when you lead so many people in so many locations.

Retail bankers never make millions out of one deal with one of their clients, but they do enjoy the certainty of many, many little deals. Just like their colleagues in a supermarket, retail bankers earn their yearly profits in cents and quarters. That can add up to many millions too. And once you have got the matching process in order, it is pretty safe and low-risk too.

When a retail banker talks of meeting clients today, he is probably seeing a focus-group of consumers or owner-operators of small or medium-sized businesses.

### So it shouldn't come as a surprise that the highest floors in most banks are not populated by retail bankers?

*Precisely.*

The alpha's, the most pro-active guys, will fight themselves to the top of the bank. Those guys that make it to the boards of the banks are generally not from retail banking. Yes, these investment or corporate bankers might express their warm interest in what goes on in retail, but their passion, their talent, their intuition isn't there. Look at the top of universal banks. How many retail bankers are in the top-200 of most of those banks? Mostly investment bankers? Disappointingly few retail bankers?

If retail bankers succeed to get on the board, quite often they are seen as slightly eccentric, not busy with *real* banking. That explains more than anything the lack of sustained, high-level interest in retail banking.

# Career paths.

**Does the career path in a bank do much for retail innovation?**
*Not really.*

For most upward mobile banking execs, retail is just a temporary and undesired break in a promising banking career. You have to put time in, so you can get the next star on your shoulders, but most can't wait "...to get back to *real* banking..." as one of my clients once told me.

The top-brass in most banks are investment or corporate bankers. That is the way up. That determines the career-ambitions.

**Is it really that bad?**
*Look around you and do the numbers in the banks that you know, Jon. How many retail-talents are there on the top floor?*

A handful? Is the route to high salaries and high bonuses faster via a long career in retail banking?

Or are the guys in retail banking viewed as just a sorry lot? Not sexy? Not with the status that the swashbuckling buccaneers of investment or corporate carry?

# Create mono-cultures.

### How can we sort out the multi-personality disorder? How can we make more of retail banking?

*Simple: cut the organisation up into mono-cultures.*

It's not rocket science, but it really works. Create independent entities which can develop and nurture their own corporate culture. Their own type of staff. Their own career-paths. Their own earning models.

It's not a cure which works only in banking. It works in all complex, multi-personality companies in all sectors.

Making your bank mono-personality should be more than just a superficial cosmetic exercise. Not just moving a few doors further down on the hall. No, it means different buildings, different career paths, different corporate personalities.

### Do we have to cut up and sell the bits?

*Not necessary, but not unlikely either.*

Think like your corporate banker friends, Jon: how would they approach a company with such devastating multi-personality disorder problems? Wouldn't they try to cut it up at the earliest possible moment? Wouldn't they suspect that the individual mono-culture bits would bring in more than the whole multi-personality giant?

Would this reasoning not work for banks?

# Synergy.

**Mono-cultures? What about synergy? That is why we are a universal bank, aren't we?**

*Synergy? Look where it brought you.*

It results in loss of control, it brings constant clashes & friction at each synergy-point. It creates constant vying for priorities in funding or IT.

That typifies a full-blown multi-personality disorder. That costs huge amounts of time & money. So, what synergy?

Didn't the unclear distinctions between retail banking and investment banking plus the unclear labelling of the risks that were pushed around spread the crisis?

**But we can never get the money as cheap as taking it from retail banking and putting it to work in investment banking, can we?**

*Your logic is like that of the gambling husband of the cleaning lady.*

The cleaning lady comes home at Friday night, worn out from her hard labor of the past week. She hangs up her coat and puts her meagre earnings on the table. Her husband gets out of his lazy chair, greets her with a his most dazzling smile, grabs the few bills off the table: "I'm off to the casino, dear, and by morning I will have doubled your money. Bye, bye!"

**We will put chinese walls in our company to set them more apart.**

*Who are you kidding?*

More often than not, they turn out to be Japanese walls; just thin paper. Ultimately it costs you valuable time. Half-baked compromises.

Which is something you can do without in the sharp, focussed, very fast Information Retail Revolution-environment.

### Such cutting up wouldn't work for banks.

*It does in South-Africa.*

The regulator doesn't allow the universal banks there. The big banking groups run totally separate companies for each banking type. There is no hanky-panky going on with unclear costing of money flows between the different companies.

Each different company is listed on the stock exchange. Which allows you to buy shares in in retail banking. Or in investment banking. Or…

# Learning mono-personalities from retail.

### Understanding consumers? Does the CEO of a supermarket chain understand customers?

*They do. They are fully aware that their earning capacity depends on it.*

The best supermarket execs that I meet have an intuitive talent for understanding the consumer and making their earning model based on that.

These supermarket execs nurture their passion for the consumer, not out of touchy-feely reasons, but because they are convinced that retail is a psychological game.

How can we make the consumer come to my stores? How can we make her buy the most when she's there, and how can we make her return & return & return?

Last but not least: how can we satisfy her with the lowest costs on our side? Which brings us to understanding people in the front-line too: how can I get the most out of my costly personnel out there?

### But in order to run a huge company you don't have to have a passion for consumers, do you? You've got people for that.

*You'll be amazed at the difference it makes.*

With the speed of developments in the Information Retail Revolution era, you have to be fast. New ideas will be over before you have even noticed them. Analysing everything till you're blue in the face will make you slow.

### We can't run a bank just by the seat of our pants, can we?

*Not just. But a trained intuition for the business you're in, makes for speedy decisions.*

Think of the story I told about the CEO of Tesco in Shanghai, he runs his huge global company by understanding what goes on in the store. By understanding consumers. In complex matters it's a shared vision and corporate intuition which make the real difference between good and bad decisions. Between failure or success.

Of course you need research, data and whatever kind of insights you can lay your hands on. Well-researched analysis can come in handy too.

But -as we all know- data and analysis tend to describe the past, and not the future.

## But we need to be big in order to get our money at the lowest costs?

*Is that so?*

I have gone through these debates with many regular retailers too. In the past decades we have experienced that supermarket chains have disinvested their own factories. In the old days they made sense, and it allowed them to source their products cheaper.

But that has changed; getting rid of them turned out to be much better. if only because for the first time they could see what a product really was costing, without the hidden costs of production, risk etc. hidden away somewhere.

## And if we have or want to hang on to the different kinds of banking?

*Create a stable of a number of mono-culture companies.*

Separate the different cultures completely, without any compromise.

Only a few regular retailers got away with hanging on to different formats under one roof. Invariably they just linked the companies at the highest level, with just a representation in a supervisory board. Plus access to global funding through a financial office.

But they make no effort whatsoever to search for any further kind of cross-company synergy. Career-lines are in the separate companies, not zigzagging in and out of corporate cultures.

**What kinds of companies are best at managing a stable of mono-culture companies?**

*Family-run companies.*

They can sometimes succeed in successfully running a stable of mono-culture companies. The corporate culture running through them is that of the generations-old culture of the family: that's how we do things here.

But don't try to duplicate such companies as the Danish Maersk group, which can run one of the largest shipping lines in the world, as well as running a number of different retail formats in Denmark.

I guess Santander is a good example in banking; a family-run company indeed.

# Governments want to cut up too.

### Regulators and governments are discussing cutting up the big banks, aren't they?

*Good idea. Wrong reason.*

They are mistaking the alarm signals of the crisis for a fundamental rethinking of the front-line of banks. The banks themselves, in the meantime, are frantically defending their multi-culture conglomerates. Whereas it doesn't take rocket science to understand that the clash of cultures within universal banks is the huge barrier for real change.

### Then what is the main reason why you want to cut up universal banks?

*A mono-corporate culture is a prerequisite for real retail-innovation.*

I have not yet seen banks or regulators that see the crisis as a call for a fundamental rethinking of banking in the Information Retail Revolution age. How to turn mis-selling to good-selling. None take a moment to lean back, and calmly rethink the retail-concepts from scratch. On the contrary, they defend the status quo.

The corporate culture in most universal banks does not stimulating retail-innovations. To say the least. Overbearing investment and corporate banking cultures make free-ranging retail innovations an uphill and slow battle.

In the wildly profitable pre-crisis days banks may have had sufficient lee-way to act slow. Not anymore. In order to operate with the necessary instinct and agility that the Information Retail Revolution requires from you, you need mono-culture banks.

# Winners and Losers.

**Looking into the future, who do you think will win?**
*Newcomers, supermarket banks, IRR giants and those banks that adopt the IRR rules the first.*

Change will come and you'll never know which new competition will succeed. But some will. Sure, the entry barriers are a bit higher in banking, when compared to music, and yes, competition may be delayed by legislators, compliance rules and other legal barriers. Soon they can enter the market with a totally clean business model, built on today's lessons, and without the big burden of all those costs. And then you'll be pretty much ...., well, you know...

**We will push them out, keep them small, or buy them.**
*In the meantime prices will be destroyed.*

A couple of years ago in Switzerland there were only two big supermarket players. Migros and Coop. They had thousands of stores. Then Aldi came in with only sixty stores. That pressed hard on prices forcing Migros and Coop up against their costs limit. All of a sudden they were old, stiff companies with huge costs, that couldn't compete with tiny agile Aldi.

**But that someone else has to become really big first, and I don't see that happening.**
*Ikea has a bank license in a number of countries, so have others.*

There are plenty of very large non-banks around, who can have a bank license within months in many countries. Don't count on that line of defence.

# Think Spermatozoids.

**Now, if we have created a mono-personality culture, how can we construct our process to keep up with the Information Retail Revolution, Hans?**

*Think spermatozoids. Of all 10.000 ideas only 1 or 2 survive. Don't bet on that 1 spermatozoid that looks promising.*

There are many new initiatives around in the IRR. From every angle new initiatives erupt. Which should you bet on? Bankers prefer to be safe and select the right new initiative.

Don't. In the Information Retail Revolution, out of a thousand initiatives, one or two will survive. That wasn't any different in the old economy, but in the Information Retail Revolution the *speed* with which these new initiatives rise and the old topple is unprecedented.

You bankers should stop lengthy and energy-wasting discussions to determine which ones will win. Or why that new player will fail. Don't think about hedging your bets. Think spermatozoids. Be agile enough to - at least- react on the 1 or 2 that will survive. But why limit yourself to reacting? Wouldn't a proactive approach be more appropriate?

Create your own cloud of initiatives. If you have an idea, you can be sure that many others are having the same at the same time. Who is to survive? No-one can say. It's a combination of being good and sheer luck. Expedia is huge, thousands of similar initiatives have died. eBay, Amazon and Facebook faced similar initiatives in their early days.

**These new initiatives cannot compete face-on with the might of us large bankers, can they?**

*They don't compete face on, Jon. That is where you are vulnerable.*

It is pretty common to downtalk new initiatives at large companies, with long histories, Jon. But that's also pretty stupid. It's like 19th century manufacturers of horse-drawn carriages moaning about those stinking cars with combustion engines: "Henry Ford will not succeed, because people love their horses."

Understand the big underlying trends and the paradigm-changes the new players are establishing. Sooner or later one will become the next eBay or Google. With a new vocabulary and grammar. At which time it will be too late for the old players to react.

## Okay so we have to be vigilant. So it is important to know which p2p lending initiative is going to win.

*Why? The point is that somebody will. Who it is, is unimportant.*

When eBay started in 1995, there were thousands of similar initiatives around. eBay, for whatever reason, pushed the right buttons at the right time. Some p2p lending vehicle will push the right buttons at the right time too.

## On which card should we bet?

*You remember Second Life?*

The buzz word of 2007: Second Life. A huge virtual world were you could lead a second life as your digital *avatar*. An avatar, just to refresh your memory, is a 3D animated person, which you style to your own liking.

In SecondLife you walk around, talk to people, build your house, and - well, eh- that was really that. But it was the new thing in 2007! Companies started opening stores in the virtual SecondLife world, trying to tap in to what was to become a huge new virtual society.

At the time I was working for a large bank. They too had seen the SecondLife future. They gathered a bunch of smart people and put together a Second Life ThinkTank. Within half a year they had created a Second Life concept. By the time the SecondLife department of this bank was operational, SecondLife was already history, a fading trend. That is typical for the IRR. New media go in and out of fashion rapidly. Speed is crucial.

## How to innovate?

*Look at how many initiatives Google takes.*

You know Google, of course. But do you know Google Labs (googlelabs.com)? You might know Google Maps, Gmail or Google Streetview. They all came from there. It's where Google tests its new ideas.

It may seem that everything Google touches turns into gold. That's not the case. Their hit rate is actually quite low, but they just launch lots of ideas. When we checked on one cold autumn day in November, 2010, Google Lab was testing 46 initiatives. I'll name a few:

Google Transliteration (phonetically type words), Indic Music Search (easy Hindi music searching), Google Scribe (a new, faster way of typing texts, something with auto correction) Walky-Talky (new mobile navigation), Google Breadcrumb (self learning applications), Image Swirl (connects images intuitively), Google Reader Play (new way to browse the internet), Fusion Tables (a service to control huge tables on the internet), Aardvark (ask any question and it will be sent to the right expert anywhere in the world) and City Tours (make walking routes through cities yourself).

The chance that Google has introduced any one of these initiatives by the time you read this book? Small. But one may be a global hit by now. They follow the spermatozoid principle.

**I agree that innovative newcomers have swept aside old molochs in other sectors. But I don't see that happening in our sector, in the financial services. We will keep them small.**

*Did you keep the private equity firms and venture capitalists small?*

Not too long ago, when a company needed money, they went to a bank. Either to take a loan, or to go to the stock exchange. In the past decades a new innovative financial service sector was created for that need. Private equity and venture capitalists have pioneered and created that new channel. In the USA that new sector is the same size as the entire banking sector.

Yes, you are involved in that sector, but does the real value-creation flow to you, the banks? Please convince me that the same cannot happen in retail banking, Jon.

## Or should we just lean back and just buy the winners of tomorrow?

*You might be too late.*

Innovation by buying was the rule at many banks. It is a strategy that has served you well in the past. In fact it was the innovation strategy for many of the largest companies in many sectors for years. You exploited your financial might to suck up those spermatozoids which had proven to grow into new life.

Just talk to your colleagues at those former molochs of the porn, music or newspaper sectors now, Jon. Innovation by buying can be a dangerously slow route in the rapidly moving Information Retail Revolution times!

## What can we learn from all of this?

*Think spermatozoids.*

Create speed, agility, and be as amorphous as the Information Retail Revolution requires. Don't bet on that one spermatozoid. Gust out large amounts of ideas at once, and celebrate when one hits the goal. Just like, well, spermatozoids.

## Part 7: Conclusion.
# Time to rethink your business model.

The Information Retail Revolution is here to stay. Exploit the new tools and conventions it offers. Not only out of defensive reasons. Use them to innovate and go on the offense. The benefits can be enormous.

Learn from other sectors how to create a larger footprint, with more sales power, at far less cost. And prevent crisis no.2 too.

What are we waiting for? If *now* is not the time to rethink your business model, *when* is it?

# The main 5 take-aways from this book.

### Retail banks do not live on an island.

The hard-hitting Information Retail Revolution has produced a new set of tools and a paradigm shift, which has caused many traditional retail models to topple. This will affect banking too.

### Apply the Information Retail Revolution in advice too.

Retail banks have embraced the tools of the Information Retail Revolution in transactional banking to the great benefit of both the client and themselves. Not on the advisory side however. This lead to structural mis-selling and to the first crisis.

### Use the Information Retail Revolution tools.

The new tools of the Information Retail Revolution are ideal for retail banks. They can increase value enormously at much lower costs. They can bring consumer-centric good-selling at much lower costs. And prevent crisis no.2.

### Re-invent Brick & mortar.

Information retailers -including banks- re-invent the function of brick & mortar & human interface in the advice, sales or maintenance phases of products for a well-defined function in the mix. Or discontinue them.

### Re-engineer yourselves for mono-personality corporate cultures.

The multi-personality disorder of banks is the barrier to a consumer-centric attitude which is a necessity for the re-invention in the Information Retail Revolution. The same disorder inhibits the necessary agility and speed.

# And:

## What did you do to write this book?

*I talked, read, analysed, looked back, digested & distilled.*

In the past months I did a lot of new research, and looked at what was happening in my projects for non-bankers. I looked back on the many retail banking projects we did in many countries since 1989. Analysed what trends I saw and what I could learn from the past.

I looked forward too. We jumped in and out of the sector to see what banking will look like in the future. We looked at what is happening in many other retail sectors. Especially information retailers like porn, music, books, travel, and a number of other retail sectors where the core-merchandise is information.

Or those sectors which may still *trade* in tangible products, but where in many parts of their value chain information technology is taking over from tangible instruments. Like cars, gambling, health-care, and yes, banking.

I talked with many bankers and with many non-bankers.

And I talked and wrote at length with my son Rik, who has graduated in digital media design and works in advertising, which allows him the latest insights in the world of new media. His age (25) forced new insights and perspectives on me too.

During the process, a common thread became visible, and various gut feelings started to interconnect and show useful patterns. Some quite startling new insights grew on me. These sharpened the trends and sharpened the lessons of the past decades.

That's how we did it.

# Track record of Eysink Smeets in banking.

Here some names of banks and other financial services companies that we worked for. Not all companies we worked for are on this list, due to confidentiality requirements.

## General banks

ING Bank / World-wide, Jyske Bank / Denmark, Den Danske Bank / Denmark, Banesto / Spain, Barnett Bank / USA, Citibank / USA DnB Nor / Norway, Nordea / Sweden, Argentaria / Spain, BBVA / Spain, Rabobank / The Netherlands, ABN Amro / The Netherlands, RCS / South Africa, Mr. Price Financial Services/ South Africa, Sainsbury's Bank / UK, Western Union/ World-wide, Volkswagen Bank / Germany/ The Netherlands, Hema Financial Services / The Netherlands, ING Direct/ World-wide Robeco / The Netherlands, De Hypotheker / The Netherlands., Postbank / The Netherlands, TNT Post / The Netherlands, Post/ Denmark, Postbanken / Norway, Post & Postbanken / Sweden, Die Post / Switzerland, New Zealand Post / New Zealand, Deutsche Post / Germany

Hans Eysink Smeets
Eysink Smeets Business Consultants BV
Singel 26, 1015 AA  Amsterdam, the Netherlands.
hans@eysinksmeets.com
www.eysinksmeets.com

www.pornforbankers.com

**Porn for bankers.** What bankers can learn from porn.